KOSHER CUISINE
FOR A NEW GENERATION

KOSHER CUISINE

FOR A **NEW** GENERATION

CANTOR MITCH

The Singing Chef

RED PORTAL PRESS

AN IMPRINT OF SCARLETTA

MINNEAPOLIS, MINNESOTA

Library of Congress Cataloging-in-Publication Data
Mitch, Cantor.
Kosher cuisine for a new generation / Cantor, Mitch.
     page   cm
Includes bibliographical references and index.
ISBN 978-1-938063-53-4 (pbk. : alk. paper) — ISBN 978-1-938063-54-1 (ebook : alk. paper)
1. Jewish cooking. I. Title.
TX724.M59 2014 641.5'676—DC23

                                                                              2014009881

Design and Production: Mighty Media, Inc., Minneapolis, MN
Cover: Aaron DeYoe   Interior: Chris Long
Editor: Alex Kuskowski

Photo Credits—Adrian Danciu: pages 5, 22, 30, 34, 46, 50, 52, 88, 96, 125, 151, 162
Brenda Piekarski: pages 14, 16, 48, 54, 56, 64, 66, 68, 73, 76, 122, 126, 132, 134, 138, 142
Matthew Winchell: pages 8, 13, 20, 22, 27, 32, 37, 58, 78, 80, 83, 84, 86, 87, 94, 108, 109, 119
Personal and family photographs supplied by author and other additional images licensed from Shutterstock.

Distributed by Publishers Group West
Printed in Canada

 A note about the QR codes used in this book: Download a free mobile app and scan the image! It will direct you to specific videos or songs at www.cantormitch.com.

CONTENTS

vii DEDICATION

1 INTRODUCTION

11 STARTERS

21 SOUPS

33 ENTRÉES
33 MEAT
45 CHICKEN
61 FISH

79 QUICHE

89 VEGETABLES

99 SAUCES

107 SALADS

115 PIES

123 SORBETS

131 BUBBIE THE BAKER
(SWEET BREADS
AND DESSERTS)

147 BUBBIE'S JEWISH
RECIPES

148 FOR PASSOVER
153 FOR SHABBAT AND
HOLIDAYS

Dedication

Without Marie and Irv, members of the Greatest Generation, who raised me with love, understanding, and high expectations, I would not be the kosher ham that I am today. My children, Joshua, Michael, and Shelly are part of a new generation. They have always believed in me and stood by me through thick and thin. They have listened to their Abba sing through decades of services. Now that's love! Susie continues to be a true inspiration. She puts up with all my shtick while showing me great love and affection. I would like to dedicate this book to them and to the generations of people yet to come. We are part of a chain made up of the past, the present, and the future. May the links we forge be strong and built on the wisdom of those who came before us.

INTRODUCTION

When I was ten years old my parents and I took a trip to Miami to visit relatives. From the backseat of the car I listened to them sing songs they loved. My dad really couldn't carry a tune, but singing with my mom he wasn't so bad! After a few minutes, I decided to join in. They were having so much fun and I wanted to be part of it. With a big voice, I let it all out! My father almost immediately pulled the car to the side of the road. My mom looked at my dad, my dad looked at my mom, and they both turned to look at me. Then they said the words I will remember for the rest of my life. "My God, you can really sing!" You could say my singing career began on that day!

You might ask, "What does singing have to do with cooking and keeping kosher?" The answer is everything!

As a teenager, I would come home to the delightful smell of the meal my mom was making for dinner. I would always ask, "What are we eating tonight?" One day after telling me what she was cooking up she said, "Taste this. What do you think it needs?" From then on, I started to help her with dinner after school. I was always so happy I would start singing while we cooked.

(Opposite): Cantor Mitch never travels far without his two favorite insturments:
his voice and his guitar!

After my bar mitzvah I was asked to join my synagogue choir. As a teenager, I found spirituality through Jewish music. For me it was a direct path to God. Nothing I do in my life today is possible without the help of God. And everything I do has spirituality within it. Whether singing, playing an instrument, worshiping, or preparing a meal, everything connects to God.

There is a phrase found in Eastern philosophy, "Mind, body, and spirit." It forms a triangle that is unbroken. I didn't know it as a teenager, but I was making my own triangle: music, spirituality, and food. They are all a part of me. My faith in God, my musical talents, and my love for food are the three most important things, aside from family, in my life. That is why I describe myself not just as Mitch, but **Cantor Mitch, the Singing Chef**. *It is my great pleasure to combine my triangle of belief to give you a fun and exciting cookbook.*

Cooking kosher food for a new generation sums up my cooking philosophy. Cooking is about moving forward while staying connected to the past, and having fun while you're at it! Kosher dishes don't have to be boring, unhealthy, or tasteless. **In fact, you do not have to be Jewish to enjoy the recipes in this book**. *In this book I have created artful, healthy, and creative recipes that I believe you will love and that are a joy to cook and serve to anyone.*

People often ask me, "Why keep kosher?" To me, it is about having a conscience. Keeping kosher is being accountable for everything that you put into your mouth. As a society we buy our weekly groceries without thought of the farmers and animals that give us sustenance. That is why Judaism stresses the word brachot, or blessings. We should strive to be thankful people, be grateful for what we have, and appreciate the abundance in our lives. Every time I sit down to a meal I say a short blessing. Saying a blessing before eating is one way to give thanks and acknowledge our part in the greater scheme of life. This kosher book is all about helping those who want to make eating a holy and thoughtful act to participate in every day.

Many of the recipes included in this book are not traditional kosher recipes. Traditional recipes, though delicious, can be time consuming and are often made from scratch. I encourage you to buy premade items that have a kosher heckcher, or a "U" on the label, which signifies rabbinical supervision in the creation of that product. It will help you keep making Mama's brisket and kugal one night, and chicken Florentine with broccoli and a sauce the next!

I felt compelled to write this book, not because I necessarily wanted to do it, but because something inside said I had to. Usually, I would much rather cook and sing than write about doing those things. However, this book has been a joy to write. I hope and pray it is also a joy to read! I am so excited to share my recipes, thoughts, and music with you. Food, music, and spirituality all go together and enhance each other. They are creative and fun. To combine all these things is my goal in **Kosher Cuisine for a New Generation**. *My dream is that this new generation will incorporate music and fun in their lives. Hopefully, they will make some of these recipes into traditions of their own.*

Once you turn the page, get ready to have fun. Pick up a knife, and start chopping! There are delightful smells coming from the kitchens of this new generation!

CANTOR MITCH

Definitions

KOSHER AND KASHRUT: The word kosher is defined as fit or perfect. Today, the word kosher refers to foods that are fit to be eaten according to Jewish dietary law.

Kashrut is the name for the set of dietary laws that define what foods are kosher. The Kashrut lists forbidden foods as foods that are said to be unhealthy for various reasons.

Kashrut codifies a distinction between fish and meat. This law prohibits the mixing of meat and milk, but does not forbid the mixing of milk and fish.

The main reason for eating kosher is found in the Torah. The Torah stresses holiness in regard to what people put in their mouths. Everything can be holy, and eating is something people do a lot! And, boy, do we love it! This book is written for those who love to eat and want to create holiness in everyday life through food.

PARVE: Parve is a Yiddish word meaning neutral. Foods that are not meat or dairy and do not have any derivatives of either product are called parve. Parve products may be used in meat or dairy meals. Parve foods include fish, foods that grow in the earth, as well as some non-dairy creamers, artificial sweeteners, and margarine.

ABBA: A Hebrew word for father.

BRACHOT: A Hebrew word for blessings that are either spoken or sung.

BUBBIE: A Yiddish word for grandmother.

FLEISHIG: A Yiddish word meaning meat or meat products.

MILCHIG: A Yiddish word meaning milk or dairy products.

ZADDIE: A Yiddish word for grandfather.

Music and Song Pairings

How many times have you sat the table with your family and sung together? A few years ago I had the pleasure of visiting my children at Jewish summer camp. The campers all said blessings before and after meals. Blessings were sung with hands banging on the tables! Imagine listening to a few hundred kids sitting around tables singing to their hearts' content. I knew that kind of fun should not be limited to camp.

Since then I have incorporated music in my home. My children are fans of modern rap music. I once improvised a rap about each dish on the table. I wanted to show my kids that their dad was hip. The kids thought I had lost my mind! Their laughter and joy in those moments were priceless.

You can do this in your own home. Whether you are Jewish or not, break into song and have fun around your table! Don't use the excuse of being too busy or in a rush. Don't be afraid to try crazy new things. Music is a powerful tool that joins people and families together. To help tie music and food together in this book, I have paired songs with dishes that match in character and flavor. Music increases family involvement around the table and around the house.

When you are preparing food you can put on a song that will lead to inspiration. While you are reading through the cookbook or eating a meal put on some great music and get your family singing along with you!

One of my favorite lines from Psalm 149:1 says, "Halleluiah! Shiru L' Adoni Shir Hadash" "Halleluiah! Sing a new song to Adoni." Sing it, rap it, or dance it to bring your family and friends together.

A meal with Cantor Mitch always comes with a side of music!

Brachot

FOR EATING BREAD
"Baruch Atah Adoni Elohenu Melech Ha'olam Ha'motzi Lechem Min Ha'aretz."

Blessed are You, Lord our God, King of the universe who brings forth bread from the earth.

FOR EATING GRAIN PRODUCTS, SUCH AS BARLEY, OATS OR WHEAT
"Baruch Atah Adoni Elohenu Melech Ha'olam Borei Minei Mezonot."

Blessed are You, Lord our God, King of the universe who creates different types of nourishment.

Cantor Mitch recieved his cantorial degree over 25 years ago. He still loves singing liturgical music.

FOR DRINKING WINE AND GRAPE JUICE

"Baruch Atah Adoni Elohenu Melech Ha'olam Borei P'ri Ha-gafen."

Blessed are You, Lord our God, King of the universe who creates fruit of the vine.

FOR EATING FRUIT FROM THE TREES

"Baruch Atah Adoni Elohenu Melech Ha'olam Borei P'ri Ha-etz."

Blessed are You, Lord our God, King of the universe who creates fruit of the trees.

FOR EATING VEGETABLES

"Baruch Atah Adoni Elohenu Melech Ha'olam Borei P'ri Ha-adamah."

Blessed are You, Lord our God, King of the universe who creates fruits of the ground.

FOR DRINKS OTHER THAN WINE FROM GRAPES

"Baruch Atah Adoni Elohenu Melech Ha'olam Shehakol Ni'he'yah Bid'varo."

Blessed are You, Lord our God, King of the universe that everything came into being through His word.

PRESENTATION

started my food career in New York as a vegetable cutter for a chain of Japanese restaurants. My training began with a cleaver and a French knife. For the cuisine I prepared, presentation was everything. Even the angles at which I cut the garnishing vegetables were essential to the overall look of a dish. I worked for about two years and must have cut more than 2,000 pounds of vegetables! I learned quickly that the way a dish is presented is just as important as the taste of the food on the plate.

Presentation is not difficult. You can place food in circles, rectangles, or triangles. You can use colors, shapes, and textures. It is simple with just a few tips.

You don't have to be a professional to create a beautiful dish. Look at the examples of food presentation throughout this book. Good presentation is done in stages without much effort. The next time you make a meal for family, friends, or just for yourself, take a moment to make it beautiful.

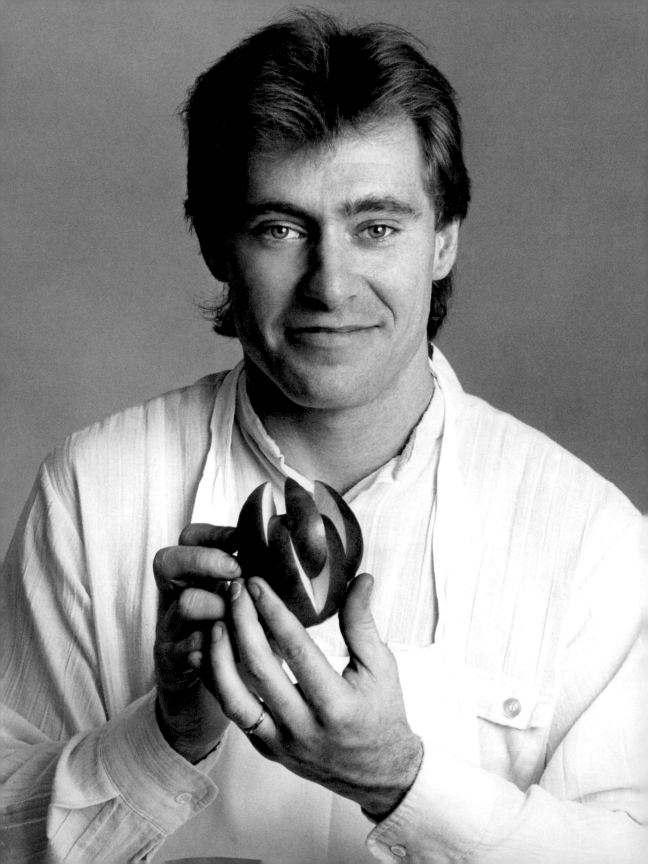

STARTERS

Good books have a beginning, middle, and end. The same can be said of good meals. The first course of any meal, the starter, is an important beginning. Starters awaken your taste buds and set the tone for the rest of the meal.

The popularity of starters is stronger than ever. Starters are easy to prepare and a great way to break the ice. That's not all they do. Many times two or three starters can make a wonderful meal. Even better, starters can be so much more than salads. Vegetables, fruits, cheeses, or soups—there are many variations to serve! Try making a starter meal one night a week. You can serve a soup and salad, some fruit and cheese, or even vegetables with crackers.

Two of my favorite starters in this book are the Vegetarian Egg Rolls and the Spiced Breaded Zucchini. In fact, they're so popular with my dinner guests I often have to remind them to save room for the entrée! So, the next time you think about starting with a salad, instead change things up. Be creative and have fun. Think outside of the box!

Remember when keeping kosher, a milk starter must be accompanied by a vegetarian or milk meal. A meat dish should never be mixed with a milk dish.

(Opposite): Cantor Mitch perfected his cooking craft over ten years while in New York. He worked as vegetable cutter, prep chef, and sous chef.

Assorted Garden Vegetable Sunrise

SONG PAIRING: "Oh, What a Beautiful Mornin'" from *Oklahoma*.

Yield: 4–6 servings

INGREDIENTS

4 leaves leaf lettuce
1 large head broccoli,
    chopped into florets
2 zucchini, thinly sliced
1 cucumber, thinly sliced
2 radishes, thinly sliced

1 red, yellow or green pepper,
    cut into strips
1 celery stalk, cut into 4-inch strips
2 cups cherry tomatoes
Ranch dressing or raspberry vinaigrette
for dipping

1. Arrange the lettuce in a bed on a serving plate.

2. Place the assorted cuts of broccoli, zucchini, cucumber, peppers, celery, and cherry tomatoes on the lettuce. Arrange the vegetables in a delicious display.

3. Put the ranch dressing or raspberry vinaigrette in a small bowl for dipping. Serve with the vegetables.

Assorted Fruits and Cheeses

Yield: 2–4 servings

INGREDIENTS

2 cups radicchio leaves

1 banana

2 apples

2 oranges

4 cups grapes

2 cups strawberries

½ pound sliced cheddar, Swiss,
   smoked Gouda, pepper jack, or Brie

½ cup Greek vanilla yogurt

1. Arrange the radicchio in a bed on a serving plate. Put the fruits on top of the leaves in the center of the plate.

2. Arrange the cheese in a circle around the outside, surrounding the fruits.

3. Put the yogurt in a small bowl for dipping. Serve with the fruits and cheeses.

Stuffed Mushrooms Florentine

 SONG PAIRING: "That's Amore" sung by Dean Martin.

Yield: 8–10 servings

Serving Suggestion: You can substitute rice for the breadcrumbs in the stuffing. It's all good!

With a fleishig meal use the same amount of olive oil or parve margarine as a nondairy substitute for the butter. Garnish the dish with diced parsley instead of Parmesan cheese.

INGREDIENTS

½ cup butter, plus extra for
   greasing the baking sheet
8–10 large mushrooms
½ cup diced onion
2 cups chopped spinach

1 tablespoon salt
1 tablespoon ground black pepper
1 tablespoon garlic powder
1 cup Italian breadcrumbs or cooked rice
Mozzarella and Parmesan cheese,
   for garnish

1. Preheat the oven to 375 degrees. Grease the baking sheet with butter.

2. Wash the mushrooms and remove the stems. Place the mushroom caps on the baking sheet.

3. In a sauté pan, combine the butter, mushroom stems, onion, spinach, salt, ground black pepper, garlic powder, and Italian breadcrumbs. Sauté over medium heat for 3 minutes.

4. Put the mixture in a blender or food processor. Pulse a few times until the mixture is smooth. Do not over blend!

5. Stuff the mushroom caps with the mixture.

6. Bake for 10 minutes. Garnish the mushrooms with Mozzarella and Parmesan cheese.

Vegetarian Egg Rolls

 SONG PAIRING: "Bali Ha'i" from the musical and movie *South Pacific*.

Yield: 6–8 servings

INGREDIENTS

½ cup finely chopped celery
5 finely chopped scallions
½ cup chopped water chestnuts
2 cloves garlic, chopped
1 tablespoon powdered ginger
2 tablespoons white sugar
¼ cup vegetable stock
1 cup shredded cabbage
½ cup soy sauce

5 tablespoons olive oil,
    plus more for frying
2 tablespoons flour
½ teaspoon salt
egg roll wraps
    (available at the grocery store)
sweet and sour sauce, mustard
    or ranch dressing for dipping

1. In a bowl, combine the celery, scallions, water chestnuts, garlic, ginger, white sugar, vegetable stock, shredded cabbage, and soy sauce.

2. In a skillet pan, warm the oil over low heat. When hot, stir in the chopped vegetable mixture. Sauté over medium heat for 3 minutes. Remove from the heat and let cool.

3. In a bowl, combine the flour, salt, and 4 tablespoons cold water to make a paste.

4. Spread out an egg roll wrap. Place 4 tablespoons of filling in the center. Fold the filled wrap like an envelope. Seal the last flap with the paste. Make egg roll wraps until the filling runs out.

5. Fill a sauté pan 1 inch deep with oil. Fry the egg rolls over high heat in small batches. Turn the egg rolls every 30 seconds. Fry time should be 2 minutes.

6. Place egg rolls on paper towels. Allow excess oil to drain before serving. Serve with sweet and sour sauce!

Why do Jewish people love Chinese food so much? Maybe because these rolls are so tasty!

Spiced Breaded Zucchini

Yield: 2–4 servings

Serving Suggestion: Serve with a ranch dip for a milk meal.

INGREDIENTS

4 zucchinis	1 teaspoon garlic powder
¼ cup orange or lemon juice	1 teaspoon dry mustard
2 cups flour	1 teaspoon basil
1 teaspoon salt	2 cups olive oil
1 teaspoon ground black pepper	¼ cup orange or lemon juice

1. Cut the zucchini into 3-inch long by ½-inch wide strips and lay them on a plate. Coat the zucchini in the orange juice.

2. In a small bowl, combine flour, salt, ground black pepper, garlic powder, dry mustard, and basil.

3. Coat the zucchini strips in the flour mixture.

4. In a sauté pan, warm the oil over medium heat. When hot, place the zucchini in the pan. Sauté for 2 to 3 minutes, or until zucchini is golden brown.

Mozzarella Avocado Brochette

Yield: 2–4 servings

INGREDIENTS
1 French bread loaf
4-6 slices mozzarella cheese
¼ cup butter
1 teaspoon salt
1 tablespoon garlic powder
3 Roma tomatoes, thinly sliced
2 avocados, thinly sliced
1 small bunch Italian parsley

1. Set the oven to broil. Cut the bread into 1 inch slices. Put the bread on a cooking sheet. Broil the bread for 1 minute on each side.

2. In a small bowl, melt the butter in the microwave. Stir in the salt and garlic powder.

3. Coat the bread slices with butter mixture. Put the cheese slices on top of the bread. Broil the bread for 1 minute and remove.

4. Place avocado and tomato slices on top of mozzarella toast. Garnish each with Italian parsley.

SOUPS

People from all parts of the world love soup. Hot or cold, creamy or clear, the popularity of soup cannot be denied. My great love for soups began while I worked in restaurants between performing off Broadway shows in New York City. I prepared two soups daily for one restaurant. I loved the challenge of coming up with something new each day.

I still love making new soups! During the winter months many of my meals consist of soup and salad. Soups are nutritious, colorful, and come in a variety of textures. There are so many variations for soup bases: beans, lentils, meats, vegetables, creams ... the list goes on and on!

My personal favorite is Jewish Chicken Soup. In fact, it's so good, sometimes my family refers to it as Jewish penicillin! But all soups seem to have that ability to help you feel better when you are under the weather. How or why, I don't know. In this section I am giving you my favorite feel good soups! Don't limit yourself to just one. Check them all out!

Serve soups in a mug with some veggies or with fruit and bread on the side.

(Opposite): The beginnings of Mama's Jewish Chicken Soup on page 27.

Southern Mushroom Cream Soup

 SONG PAIRING: "Dixie" "Look away! Look away! Look away! Dixie Land."

Yield: 6–8 servings

Serving Suggestion: To kick up the flavor index add more spices I have listed or maybe some of your own!

INGREDIENTS
½ cup butter
2 cups chopped onion
2 cups chopped celery
2 tablespoons garlic powder
1 teaspoon ground black pepper
2 tablespoons salt
4–6 cups sliced mushrooms
4 cups vegetable stock
4 cups milk
4 cups half and half
½ cup cooking sherry (optional)

1. In a soup pot over medium heat melt butter. Stir in the onion and celery. Sauté ingredients for 5 minutes.

2. Stir in the garlic powder, ground black pepper, and salt. Turn the heat to low and cook for 10 minutes.

3. Remove the cooked onion mixture from the pot. Place the mixture and mushrooms in a blender or food processor. Blend until the mixture is smooth.

4. Return the blended mixture to the pot. Stir in the vegetable stock, milk, half and half, and sherry. Simmer over low heat for 30 minutes.

5. Stir the soup. Simmer for another 30 minutes. Stir again before serving.

Tomato and Herb Provençal Soup

 SONG PAIRING: "Moonlight in Vermont." Frank Sinatra made this song popular.

Yield: 4–6 servings

For chunky style soup, serve the soup immediately after simmering. For a cream style soup, add 2 cups half and half.

INGREDIENTS

½ cup butter if using vegetable stock
    parve margarine if using chicken stock
4 cups diced tomatoes
2 cups diced onions
1 cup diced scallion
1 cup diced celery
1 cup kosher chicken stock

3 (10.5 ounce) cans tomato soup
2 tablespoons parsley
1 tablespoon rosemary
1 tablespoon Herbs de Provence
    or oregano
½ cup white cooking wine
parsley and cilantro, for garnish

1. In a soup pot over low heat melt the butter. Stir in the tomatoes, onions, scallions, and celery. Cook ingredients over medium heat for 10 minutes, stirring every 2 minutes.

2. Stir in the chicken or vegetable stock, tomato soup, parsley, rosemary, Herbs de Provence, and white cooking wine. Simmer the soup for 30 minutes.

3. Put the soup in a blender or food processor. Pulse on the blend setting until smooth.

4. Garnish the soup with parsley and cilantro.

Herbs de Provence is a type of dried herb mixture in southeastern France. It is a popular blend that can be used to season meat, poultry, or vegetable dishes.

Vegetable Pot Luck Soup

 SONG PAIRING: "Over the Rainbow" from *The Wizard of Oz*.

Yield: 6–8 servings

INGREDIENTS

5 cups assorted vegetables, diced
½ cup butter
4 cups canned tomato soup
3 cups chicken stock or vegetable stock
½ cup Marcella cooking wine or red wine
    or white wine
1 tablespoon salt
1 tablespoon ground black pepper
1 tablespoon oregano

Here's an easy soup to prepare with leftover vegetables! Feel free to use any or all of the following vegetables in the soup: onion, scallions, red or green pepper, carrots, zucchini, parsley, potato, peas, corn, and tomatoes.

1. In a large saucepan, combine the assorted vegetables and butter. Cook over medium heat for 5 to 7 minutes, stirring constantly.

2. Stir in the tomato soup, chicken stock, and wine.

3. Stir in the salt, ground black pepper, and oregano. Cook the soup over low heat for 1 hour.

Louisiana Black Bean Soup

 SONG PAIRING: "When the Saints Go Marching In."

Yield: 8–10 servings

Serving Suggestion: For garnish, try using sour cream, lemon slices, or parsley.

INGREDIENTS

2 cups diced onion

1 cup diced celery

1/3 cup chopped parsley

2 cups vegetable stock

¼ cup butter

1 tablespoon salt

1 tablespoon ground black pepper

1 tablespoon garlic powder

4 tablespoons cooking sherry

4 (15 ounce) cans black beans

1. In a large pot combine the onion, celery, parsley, vegetable stock, butter, salt, ground black pepper, garlic powder, and sherry. Cook the ingredients over medium heat for 5 to 7 minutes, stirring every 2 minutes.

2. Stir in the black beans. Simmer for 45 minutes, stirring every 5 to 10 minutes. Garnish, if desired, before serving.

Mama's Jewish Chicken Soup

 SONG PAIRING: "Tradition" from *Fiddler on the Roof*.

Yield: 8–12 servings

INGREDIENTS

1 whole kosher chicken
1 large diced onion
3 carrots, thinly sliced
1 stalk celery, thinly sliced
1 head parsley, diced
1 clove garlic, crushed and diced
¼ cup olive oil

8 cups kosher chicken stock
2 tablespoons salt
1 tablespoon ground black pepper
1 tablespoon rosemary
1 tablespoon savory
2 bay leaves

1. Wash the chicken under cold water. Pat to dry.

2. In a large soup pot combine all of the ingredients. Simmer over low heat for 2 hours, stirring every 30 minutes.

3. Remove the chicken from the pot. Take the meat off the bone using a knife. Chop the chicken meat into bite sized pieces. Add the chopped chicken to the pot.

4. Simmer the soup for 30 minutes.

I don't know about you, but this soup does the trick when I have a cold or the flu. It's the Jewish penicillin. I have even heard doctors say it is just as good as an antibiotic! Okay, maybe not. But a good cup of soup never hurts, and it feels good in your tummy.

Cantor's Cold Gazpacho

 SONG PAIRING: "America" or "Let's Rumble!" from *West Side Story*

Yield: 4–6 servings

Wait until summer to try this gazpacho soup. It will cool down even the hot head in your family!

INGREDIENTS
2 cucumbers, peeled and seeded
3 (16 ounce) cans stewed tomatoes
2 cups vegetable stock
1 cup diced fresh parsley
½ lemon, cut into sections
2 tablespoons olive oil
2 tablespoons chopped chives
salt and ground black pepper, to taste

1. Put the cucumbers, tomatoes, vegetable stock, parsley, and lemon in a blender or food processor. Blend the ingredients together coarsely. Empty the ingredients into a mixing bowl.

2. Add the olive oil and chives to the bowl. Stir to mix. Season the soup to taste with salt and ground black pepper.

3. Refrigerate the soup for 2 hours.

Vichyssoise

 SONG PAIRING: "Cabaret," the theme song from *Cabaret*.

Yield: 4–6 servings

Serving Suggestion: This soup may be served hot or cold.

INGREDIENTS

3 leeks, chopped

1 onion, chopped

4 tablespoons butter or olive oil

5 medium potatoes, peeled and
   thinly sliced

4 cups vegetable stock

2 cups half and half

salt and ground black pepper, to taste

¼ cup chopped chives or watercress
   for garnish, if desired

1. In a medium pan, combine the leeks, onion, and butter. Sauté the ingredients over medium heat for 3 minutes.

2. Stir in the potatoes, vegetable stock, half and half, and chives. Add salt and ground black pepper to the soup to taste.

3. Simmer the soup for 1 hour. Take off heat. Let the soup cool.

4. Put the soup in a blender or food processor. Blend on low until smooth. Reheat the soup over low heat for hot soup, or chill for 30 minutes for cold soup.

5. Before serving garnish with chives, parsley, or watercress.

Cream of Asparagus Soup

Yield: 4–6 servings

INGREDIENTS

4–5 cups asparagus, cut into
   1-inch pieces
1/2 cup butter
2 cups chopped onion
2 cups vegetable stock
2 cups half and half
1 cup milk

1 teaspoon salt
1 teaspoon ground black pepper
1 tablespoon garlic powder
6 small sprigs fresh dill, for garnish
½ teaspoon paprika, for garnish
¼ cup grated Parmesan cheese,
   for garnish

1. In a microwave safe container, put asparagus and 1 cup water. Microwave for 3 minutes on high. Drain the water and set aside.

2. In a soup pot, melt the butter over medium heat. When melted, add onion and sauté for 2 minutes.

3. In the pot, stir in the asparagus, vegetable stock, half and half, milk, salt, ground black pepper, garlic powder, and dill. Simmer for 10 minutes. Remove from heat and let it cool for 10 minutes.

4. Put the soup in a blender or food processor. Pulse until smooth. Return the soup to the soup pot. Cook over low heat for 15 to 20 minutes, stirring every 5 minutes.

5. Garnish with fresh dill, grated cheese or paprika just before serving.

Cream of Broccoli Soup

Yield: 4–6 servings

INGREDIENTS

4 cups broccoli florets
2 cups vegetable stock
2 cups half and half
1 cup milk
1 teaspoon salt
1 teaspoon ground black pepper
1 teaspoon garlic powder

1 tablespoon Herbs de Provence
½ cup butter
2 cups chopped onion
1 bunch parsley, for garnish
6 thin slices red pepper, for garnish
¼ cup grated Parmesan cheese,
    for garnish
mint leaves, for garnish

1. In a microwave safe container, put broccoli and 1 cup water. Microwave for 3 minutes on high. Drain the water and set aside.

2. In a soup pot, melt the butter over medium heat. When melted, add onion and sauté for 2 minutes.

3. In the pot, stir in the broccoli, vegetable stock, half and half, milk, salt, ground black pepper, garlic powder, and Herbs de Provence. Simmer for 10 minutes. Remove from heat and let it cool for 10 minutes.

4. Put the soup in a blender or food processor. Pulse until smooth. Return the soup to the soup pot. Cook over low heat for 15 to 20 minutes, stirring every 5 minutes.

5. Garnish with parsley, grated cheese or thin slices of red pepper just before serving.

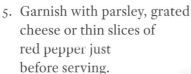

ENTRÉES

The entrée is the main course of the meal. Whether beef, chicken, fish or pasta, entrées fill you up! When looking at a menu, it is usually the entrée section the eye is first drawn to. It is the entrée that we remember. The presentation, flavor, and size are what make an impression!

The entrée recipes I have included here are easy to prepare and, of course, kosher! So I say, "Why go out?" Make it at home. Enjoy great food in the comfort of your home with family and friends.

> Enjoy meats with vegetables, eggs, fish, or fruit. Just save the foods containing dairy for milchig meals.

MEAT

To keep kosher while eating a fleishig meal, start by purchasing kosher meal! Kosher meat is more available than ever. Whether shopping for ground beef, brisket or steak, many stores now offer a kosher meat

(Opposite): Brisket is just right for Shabbat!

section. You may find it a bit more expensive. All kosher meat must be slaughtered under humane conditions and under strict rabbinical supervision. In the process, the blood has been drained and the meat has been salted to ensure that the most amount of blood has been removed.

I enjoy preparing the recipes in this section and I think you will too. The first time I made Abba Burgers my family could barely get their mouths around the bun, but that didn't stop them. It was a thick, delicious kosher burger, and they loved it! The Shabbat Brisket is one traditional Jewish meat recipe that came from Bubbie. It is a truly delectable staple of a traditional Sabbath meal. Explore the other easy recipes in this section to find your kosher meat fix.

Remember most meat must be rinsed with water to remove the excess salt from the koshering process. Ground meat and fish are the only exceptions. They do not need to be rinsed.

Green Pepper Steak

 SONG PAIRING: "Chicago" from the musical *Chicago*.

Yield: 4 servings

Steaks can be broiled, fried, or grilled. I grill my steaks, but you can choose the cooking method that works best in your kitchen.

INGREDIENTS

4 (6–8 ounce) kosher steaks

2 green peppers, diced

2 onions, diced

2 tomatoes, diced

¼ cup parve margarine

salt and ground black pepper, to taste

3 bananas, sliced

1 cucumber, sliced

1 cup rum

1. Preheat the oven to broil. Wash the steak under cold water. Pat to dry.

2. Broil the steaks on a broiling pan for approximately 2 minutes on each side to cook medium well. Set aside.

3. In a medium sauté pan, combine the green peppers, onions, tomatoes, and parve margarine. Sauté the ingredients over high heat for 2 minutes. Season with salt and ground black pepper.

4. Stir in the bananas, cucumber, and rum. Simmer for an additional 5 to 7 minutes over medium heat. The alcohol will burn off during the cooking process.

5. Spoon the vegetable banana mixture over the steaks before serving.

Sweet & Sour Meatballs

 SONG PAIRING: "Ain't She Sweet?" Fats Waller made it oh, so sweet!

Yield: 6–8 servings

Serving Suggestion: Meatballs can be served over white rice or pasta.

INGREDIENTS

3 pounds kosher ground beef

1 teaspoon salt

3 teaspoons ground black pepper

1½ tablespoons garlic powder

4 slices bread, crumbled

1 (12 ounce) jar grape jelly

1 (12 ounce) bottle chili sauce

1. In a large bowl, combine the ground beef, salt, ground black pepper, garlic powder, and crumbled bread.

2. Form golf ball sized meatballs with the mixture.

3. In a medium pan, cook jelly and chili sauce over high heat until boiling. Reduce the heat to medium.

4. Add the meatballs to the pan. Cook the mixture for 60 minutes. Turn the meatballs occasionally.

Spiced Rice and Beef

 SONG PAIRING: "I Get a Kick Out of You." Frank Sinatra made this one great!

Yield: 4–6 servings

Serving Suggestion: Serve this dish with a side of vegetables.

If you want more of a kick, add 2 tablespoons of Tabasco sauce.

INGREDIENTS
2 pounds kosher ground beef
1 green, red, or yellow pepper, diced
1 (16 ounce) can diced tomatoes
1 teaspoon salt
1 teaspoon ground black pepper
1 tablespoon Herbs de Provence
    or oregano
2 tablespoons steak sauce
2 cups cooked rice

1. Preheat the oven to 350 degrees.

2. Put all the ingredients in a casserole dish. Stir to combine.

3. Bake the dish for 30 to 40 minutes.

"It's up to you, New York, New York ..."

Abba Burgers

 SONG PAIRING: "Oh My Papa" sung by Eddie Fisher.

Yield: 4–5 servings

Abba means father in Hebrew, and this burger is the father of burgers! I make these burgers big. In a bun these burgers can make it challenging to take a bite. But with a little hutzpah you can press it together, let the juices run, and have a good time! Remember, for this one you'll need plenty of napkins.

INGREDIENTS

2 pounds kosher ground beef

1 tablespoon garlic powder

1 tablespoon lemon pepper

1 tablespoon basil or rosemary leaves

1 teaspoon salt

1 large onion, diced

4 tablespoons steak sauce (optional)

1. Preheat the grill. Put all the ingredients in a bowl. Mix the ingredients together thoroughly.

2. What makes these burgers special is the size! Form only four or five burger patties from the ingredients. Each patty should be approximately 1 inch thick and 4 inches across.

3. Grill the patties for at least 3 minutes on each side.

Cantor's Jewish Sabbath Brisket

 SONG PAIRING: "Shabbat Prayer" from *Fiddler on the Roof*.

Yield: 4–6 servings

Serving Suggestion: Serve with cooked carrots and golden baby potatoes.

Shabbat is a special time. We thank God for all we have and take time to reflect. We say prayers over candles, wine, and food. We realize that everything we have does not come from us. To rest, be with friends and family, and share love is what Shabbat is really all about.

INGREDIENTS

3 pounds brisket

3 tablespoons garlic

2 medium onions, sliced

4–6 cups sliced mushrooms

2 carrots, sliced

1 envelope onion soup mix

1 teaspoon rosemary (optional)

1 teaspoon parve margarine (optional)

1. Preheat the oven to 350 degrees. Rinse the brisket under cold water. Pat to dry. Place the brisket in a roasting pan. Add the garlic, onion, mushrooms, and carrots to the pan.

2. In a bowl, combine the onion soup mix, rosemary, parve margarine, and 1 cup water. Pour the onion soup mixture over the brisket and vegetables.

3. Cover the brisket with the roasting pan lid. Bake for 1½ to 2 hours. The meat should peel back with a fork when done.

4. Cut into a small piece of brisket to see that meat is completely cooked through out. No pink meat should remain.

5. Remove brisket from the pan. Place it on a cutting board. Slice the brisket into thin cuts. Slice against the grain of the meat. Place the sliced brisket on a serving platter. Spoon vegetables and broth over the top.

Cantor's Killer Kosher Chili

Yield: 6–8 servings

Serving Suggestion: Garnish with sour cream or cheese for your non-Jewish friends. Garnish with parsley and crushed crackers for your friends who keep kosher. Serve with a side salad.

INGREDIENTS
1 pound kosher ground beef
1 large onion, diced
1 green or red pepper, diced
1 cup diced celery
3 (16 ounce) cans chili or kidney beans
1 (28 ounce) can diced tomatoes
¼ cup olive oil
3 tablespoons cumin
4 tablespoons garlic powder
6 tablespoons chili powder
3 tablespoons salt
4 tablespoons ground black pepper
¼ cup white wine

1. In a large pot combine ground beef, onion, green pepper, celery, beans, tomatoes, and oil. Stir over medium-high heat until beef is browned, about 4 to 6 minutes.

2. Reduce the heat to medium. Stir in the cumin, garlic powder, chili powder, salt, ground black pepper and white wine.

3. Cook the soup for about 15 minutes, stirring every 5 minutes.

4. Reduce heat to medium-low. Simmer the soup for 15 to 20 minutes before serving.

CHICKEN

Everyone loves chicken. Or, at least, I know I do! I eat a lot of chicken and never tire of it. Even better, there are so many ways to enjoy a cooked chicken. You can sauté it, bake it, fry it, BBQ it, even broil it. In the kosher meat section of your local store you can now find an abundance of cuts. It is a great healthy kosher meal for every occasion.

My recipes for chicken use kosher skinless breasts exclusively. Breasts are easy to prepare and have a quick cooking time. Just remember to wash the salt off the meat before preparing it. Even with using only chicken breasts as the main meat ingredient, each recipe has a unique delicious flavor that will impress your family and friends. The taste will be irresistible. No matter which recipe you choose, it will still look and taste like it came from a restaurant. Shhh, our secret!

These dishes will use parve margarine, canola oil, or olive oil to keep kosher. Remember that chicken is a type of meat. Avoid dairy products in other courses if chicken is the main dish. Desserts after a chicken meal can be fruit, fresh sorbet, or nuts.

Chicken a l'Orange

Yield: 4–6 servings

Serving Suggestion: Serve with the vegetable of your choice, rice, or pasta.

INGREDIENTS
4–5 skinless kosher chicken breasts
1 citrus fruit (orange, lemon, lime, grapefruit) for marinade
2 cups flour
1 cup breadcrumbs (optional)
2 tablespoons garlic powder
2 tablespoons oregano
1 teaspoon salt
1 teaspoon ground black pepper
1 cup parve margarine or olive oil
2 oranges, juiced
1 cup Asian glaze sauce or stir fry orange sauce

1. Wash the chicken under cold water. Pat to dry.

2. In a bowl, juice the citrus fruit. Marinate the chicken in the bowl for 6 minutes.

3. Cut each breast in half. Pound each piece until slightly flattened.

4. In a large bowl, combine the flour, breadcrumbs, garlic powder, oregano, salt, and pepper. Lightly dust the chicken in the flour mixture.

5. In a sauté pan, melt parve margarine over medium high heat. Cook the chicken in the melted margarine until golden brown on both sides. Remove the breasts from the pan. Set aside.

6. Put the orange juice and the Asian glaze sauce in the same pan. Bring the mixture to a boil over high heat. Add 1 to 2 tablespoons flour while stirring to thicken the sauce.

7. Spoon the sauce over the chicken. Garnish with curls of orange peel.

Apricot Chicken

 SONG PAIRING: "Summertime" from *Porgy and Bess.*

Yield: 4–6 servings

Serving Suggestion: Serve with vegetable of your choice, rice, or pasta.

INGREDIENTS

2 pounds kosher chicken breasts

1 citrus fruit (orange, lemon, lime, or grapefruit) for marinade

2 cups flour

1 cup breadcrumbs (optional)

1 tablespoon garlic powder

1 tablespoon sage

1 teaspoon salt

1 teaspoon ground black pepper

1 cup parve margarine or canola oil

½ cup white wine

¼ cup apricot preserves

¼ cup diced dried apricots

1. Wash the chicken under cold water. Pat to dry.

2. In a bowl, juice the citrus fruit. Marinate the chicken in the bowl for about 6 minutes.

3. Cut each breast in half. Pound each piece until slightly flattened.

4. In a bowl, combine the flour, breadcrumbs, garlic powder, sage, salt, and pepper. Lightly dust the chicken in the flour mixture.

5. In a sauté pan, melt the parve margarine over medium-high heat. Cook chicken in the pan until golden brown on both sides. Remove the breasts. Set the chicken aside.

6. Add the wine, apricot preserves, and diced apricots to the same pan. Bring the mixture to a simmer over medium heat. Stir, adding 1 to 2 teaspoons flour a little at a time to thicken the sauce. Spoon the mixture over the chicken. Garnish with pecans or walnuts, or let the sauce speak for itself!

Chicken Marsala

 SONG PAIRINGS: "Se vuol ballere" and "Non più andrai" from the *Marriage of Figaro*.

Yield: 3–4 servings

INGREDIENTS

½ cup packaged wild rice

3–4 skinless kosher chicken breasts

1 orange, juiced

1 cup thinly sliced mushrooms

½ cup chopped scallions

1½ cups parve margarine or canola oil, divided

2 cups flour

½ teaspoon salt

1 teaspoon ground black pepper

1 tablespoon garlic powder

1 tablespoon oregano

¾ cup Marsala wine

½ cup almond slivers

2 teaspoons cornstarch

1. Follow the package directions to cook the wild rice. Make sure to allow adequate time for the wild rice to fully cook.

2. Wash the chicken under cold water. Pat to dry.

3. Marinate the chicken in the orange juice for 10 minutes. Gently pound the chicken to half the original thickness.

4. In a sauté pan, combine the mushrooms, scallions, and ½ cup parve margarine. Cook over high heat for 2 minutes. Drain the contents of the sauté pan into a small bowl.

5. Lightly flour the chicken on both sides. Place the chicken in the heated sauté pan with the ¾ cup parve margarine. Cook the chicken over high heat. Cook both sides of the chicken until each piece is golden brown. Remove the chicken. Set it aside.

6. Put the remaining parve margarine, the mushroom mixture, salt, pepper, garlic powder, oregano, and wine in the same pan used to cook the chicken. Cook over high heat for about 3 minutes. Add 1 to 2 teaspoons cornstarch while stirring to thicken the mixture if needed.

7. Serve chicken breasts over a large helping of wild rice. Pour the sauce over the chicken. Top with slivered almonds.

Chicken Florentine

 SONG PAIRING: "A Man Without Love" sung by Al Martino.

Yield: 4–6 servings

Serving Suggestion: Serve with vegetables, rice, or pasta.

INGREDIENTS

3 kosher chicken breasts

2 cups flour

2 teaspoons cornstarch

¼ cup breadcrumbs

2 tablespoons garlic powder

1 teaspoon salt

1 teaspoon ground black pepper

2 tablespoons oregano

2 cups parve margarine, or olive oil

5–6 cups fresh spinach

½ cup white wine

1 lemon, juiced

1. Wash the chicken under cold water. Pat to dry. Cut the chicken breasts in half. Gently pound each half until slightly flattened.

2. In a bowl, mix the flour, breadcrumbs, garlic powder, salt, pepper, and oregano. Lightly dust the chicken breasts with flour mixture.

3. In a sauté pan, heat 1 cup parve margarine over high heat until simmering. Sauté the chicken until it is golden brown on both sides. Set cooked chicken aside.

4. In the same pan, combine ½ cup parve margarine and the spinach. Lightly sauté over medium heat, stirring the spinach until the leaves are wilted. Remove the spinach from the pan. Set it aside.

5. In the same pan, combine ½ cup parve margarine and white wine to start the sauce. Heat on high until boiling. Stir in the lemon juice and 1 to 2 teaspoons of cornstarch if needed for thickening. Whisk while simmering until sauce thickens, approximately 1 minute.

6. Make a bed of spinach on each serving plate. Place the chicken breasts on top of the spinach. Spoon the sauce over the top of each breast.

Pesto Chicken

 SONG PAIRING: "Volare" also known as "Nel blu dipinto di blu," made famous by Jerry Vale.

Yield: 4–6 servings

Serving Suggestion: Place the cooked chicken on a bed of rice or pasta.

INGREDIENTS
3 kosher chicken breasts
2 cups flour
¼ cup breadcrumbs (optional)
2 tablespoons garlic powder
1 teaspoon salt
1 teaspoon ground black pepper
2 tablespoons oregano
1 cup parve margarine or olive oil
1 (7 ounce) jar pesto

1. Wash the chicken under cold water. Pat to dry. Cut the chicken breasts in half. Gently pound each half until slightly flattened.

2. In a bowl, combine the flour, breadcrumbs, garlic powder, salt, pepper, and oregano. Lightly dust the chicken breasts with the flour mixture.

3. In a sauté pan, melt the parve margarine over high heat. Put the chicken in the pan. Sauté until the chicken is golden brown on both sides.

4. In a bowl, mix the pesto with ¼ cup hot water. Microwave for 1 minute. Spoon the pesto sauce over each chicken breast.

Spanish Chicken

 SONG PAIRING: "Macarena." This was a big hit song in the 1990's.

Yield: 3–4 servings

Serving Suggestion: Serve the chicken on top of rice or pasta.

INGREDIENTS
4 kosher skinless chicken breasts
2 cups flour
¼ cup breadcrumbs (optional)
2 tablespoons garlic powder
1 teaspoon salt
1 teaspoon ground black pepper
2 tablespoons oregano
1 cup olive oil
1 (16 ounce) jar chunky salsa
1 tablespoon cilantro
1 lime, juiced

1. Wash the chicken under cold water. Pat to dry. Cut the chicken breasts in half. Gently pound each half until slightly flattened.

2. In a bowl, combine the flour, breadcrumbs, garlic powder, salt, pepper, and oregano. Lightly dust the chicken breasts with the flour mixture.

3. In a sauté pan, heat the oil over high heat. Put the chicken in the pan. Sauté the chicken until golden brown on both sides.

4. Mix the salsa with a cilantro and lime juice. Spoon the salsa mixture over the chicken breasts just before serving.

Curry Chicken

 SONG PAIRING: "Be Our Guest" from *Beauty and the Beast*.

Yield: 3–4 servings

Serving Suggestion: Try serving the chicken over rice.

INGREDIENTS

¼ cup olive oil, canola oil
   or parve margarine
1 cup scallions
2 teaspoons garlic
1½ cup chopped carrots
½ cup chopped celery

4 cups cooked and cubed
   kosher chicken breasts
1½ cup kosher chicken broth
4 teaspoons curry powder
1 cup applesauce

1. In a saucepan, heat oil over medium heat. Stir in the scallions, garlic, carrots, and celery to the saucepan. Sauté until the scallions are clear, about 5 minutes.

2. Stir in the chicken, broth, curry, and applesauce. Bring the mixture to a boil over high heat.

3. Reduce heat to low. Simmer partially covered for 20 to 30 minutes, stirring occasionally.

Grilled Chicken Breasts

Yield: 3–4 servings

Serving Suggestion: Serve the chicken with some cooked vegetables.

Too many people take something simple and make it complex. Grilled chicken breasts are easy to prepare if you have the tools and know how.

INGREDIENTS

3–4 kosher chicken breasts

½ cup Italian dressing
    or citrus juice marinade

1 teaspoon garlic powder

1 teaspoon lemon pepper

1 teaspoon oregano

1. Preheat the grill. Wash the chicken under cold water. Pat to dry.

2. Marinate the chicken in a bowl with the dressing for 5 to 7 minutes.

3. Remove the chicken from the marinade. Sprinkle garlic powder, lemon pepper, and oregano to either side of each breast.

4. Place the chicken on the grill. Reduce the heat slightly. Turn the chicken every 5 minutes. Cook for about 7–10 minutes. Be careful you don't under or overcook! Check to see if there is any pink in the meat before removing it from the grill.

Make a citrus juice marinade.
Juice about four lemons and limes,
or juice three oranges.

FISH

Fish can be cooked many ways. You can broil, bake, sauté, fry, or poach it. That said, it is sometimes hard to get your family in the mood for fish. It is a healthy option, but a lot of people have a difficult time making it taste truly delicious.

> I work with walleye—a great Minnesota favorite—red snapper, salmon, sole, and, what I call my all-purpose fish, tilapia. You can substitute your favorite fish using the same recipes. I did not include any non-kosher fish in my recipes, but here's a helpful hint if you get creative: shark, catfish, and all shellfish are prohibited food items for those eating kosher.

With my dishes you won't struggle to feed your family something other than the packaged fish sticks from the frozen food aisle. I would put one of my fish dishes up against a package of fish sticks any day. Blindfold your kids, or someone else's kids, and let them decide. Never mind, I've already done it! My fish recipes win every time.

This section has a variety of healthy recipes to help you cook fish the way you and your family like best. The protein and good fats fish provide will keep your family healthy.

Eat and serve more fish. You will look and feel great. That's my story and I'm sticking to it!

Broiled Garlic Sole

 SONG PAIRING: "Sittin' on the Dock of the Bay" made famous by Otis Redding.

Yield: 3–4 servings

Serving Suggestion: Serve with rice or any type of vegetable.

INGREDIENTS

¼ cup olive oil

4 cloves garlic, crushed and diced

3 tablespoons lemon juice

1 teaspoon salt

4–5 sole fillets

1. Preheat the oven on broil. Brush olive oil over the broiling pan to prevent sticking. Place fish on the broiling pan.

2. In a bowl, combine the garlic, olive oil, lemon juice, and salt. Spread the garlic mixture over the fish. Let stand for 2 minutes.

3. Broil the fish for 2 to 3 minutes on one side.

Sole Almandine

 SONG PAIRING: "Yellow Submarine" by The Beatles.

Yield: 3–4 servings

Serving Suggestion: Serve the fish over rice.

INGREDIENTS

½ cup butter

1 tablespoon garlic powder

1 teaspoon salt

1 tablespoon sage

3 tablespoons lime juice

1 teaspoon almond extract

4–5 sole fillets

½ cup ground almonds

½ cup thinly sliced almonds

2–3 tablespoons parsley

1. Put ¼ cup butter in a small bowl. Melt the butter in the microwave. Stir in the garlic powder, salt, sage, lime juice, and almond extract.

2. Spoon the mixture over both sides of each sole fillet. Coat the fillets with the ground almonds.

3. In a sauté pan, melt remaining butter over medium heat. Place the fillets in the pan. Sauté each fillet until both sides are golden brown.

4. Garnish the fillets with remaining almonds and parsley.

Golden Tilapia

 SONG PAIRING: "Goldfinger," the title song from the James Bond movie.

Yield: 3–4 servings

Serving Suggestion: Serve alone or with rice and vegetables.

You can use any of the following as a great accompaniment to the fish: tartar sauce, lemon juice, hot sauce, or salad dressing.

INGREDIENTS
1 lemon, cut in half
4–5 tilapia fillets
1 teaspoons salt
1 teaspoon ground black pepper
1 tablespoon Italian seasoning
2 cups flour
2 cups canola oil

1. Squeeze a lemon half over the fillets.

2. In a bowl, combine the salt, ground black pepper, Italian seasoning, and flour. Coat each fillet in the mixture.

3. In the sauté pan, warm the oil over high heat. Test the heat of the oil by dipping a corner of the fillet in the pan. The fillet should sizzle. Carefully put each fillet in the pan.

4. Fry the fish for 1½ minutes on each side or until it is golden brown and crispy on both sides.

5. Pat the fish on paper towels to remove any excess oil.

6. Garnish with thin slices of the remaining lemon before serving.

Tilapia Alfredo

 SONG PAIRING: "O Sole Mio" sung by Mario Lanza.

Yield: 3–4 servings

Serving Suggestion: Serve the fish with rice or pasta, or over a bed of sauted spinach leaves.

This is a dish that can be broiled, fried, or baked. The easiest no-mess way is to bake!

INGREDIENTS

¼ cup olive oil, plus a tablespoon for greasing the foil

4–5 tilapia fillets

1 red pepper, diced

1 scallion, diced

1 tablespoon garlic powder

1 tablespoon salt

1 tablespoon lemon pepper

1 tablespoon Italian seasoning

1 (7 ounce) container Alfredo sauce

¼ cup grated Parmesan cheese

¼ cup diced Italian parsley

candied walnut for garnish (optional)

1. Preheat oven to 400 degrees. Line the bottom of a broiling pan with aluminum foil. Pour a tablespoon olive oil over the foil. Spread the oil over the foil evenly.

2. Place the fillets in the prepared pan. Put the red pepper and scallions into the pan.

3. In a small bowl, combine the garlic powder, salt, lemon pepper, and Italian seasoning. Sprinkle the seasoning mixture over the fillets.

4. Cover the fillets with aluminum foil. Bake for 12 minutes. Garnish with diced Italian parsley.

5. Heat sauce for 30 seconds then spoon the Alfredo sauce over the fillets. Sprinkle the Parmesan cheese over the sauce before serving.

Tilapia Al Pesto

 SONG PAIRING: "Quando Quando Quando." Tony Renis gets the nod for this one!

Yield: 3–4 servings

Serving Suggestion: Serve the fish over rice or pasta.

INGREDIENTS

¼ cup olive oil, plus more for greasing foil

4–5 tilapia fillets

1 tablespoon garlic powder

1 teaspoon salt

1 teaspoon lemon pepper

1 tablespoon Italian seasoning

1 (7 ounce) jar of pesto

¼ cup Parmesan cheese

½ lemon

1. Preheat the oven to 425 degrees. Line a 10×13-inch pan with aluminum foil. Spread a tablespoon olive oil evenly over the foil. Place the fillets in the prepared pan.

2. In a small bowl, combine the garlic powder, salt, lemon pepper, and Italian seasoning. Sprinkle the seasoning mixture over the fillets.

3. Bake the fillets for 8–10 minutes. Squeeze the lemon on the fish before serving.

4. In a small bowl, combine pesto and 4 tablespoons water. Stir the ingredients vigorously. Heat in a small saute pan or in micfrowave. Spread the pesto mixture on the fillets. Sprinkle the Parmesan cheese over the fillets before serving.

For the baked fish recipes, I use aluminum foil to line my pans. It makes for an easy cooking experience and an even easier clean up. Be sure that you cover the foil with a thin layer of olive oil, margarine, or butter.

Spanish Baked Tilapia

 SONG PAIRING: "La Bamba." Do you remember that Richie Valens hit?

Yield: 3–4 servings

Serving Suggestion: Serve the fish over rice or pasta.

INGREDIENTS

2 cups canola oil, or olive oil

4–5 tilapia fillets

1 tablespoon garlic powder

1 teaspoon salt

1 teaspoon lemon pepper

1 tablespoon Italian seasoning

2–3 heaping tablespoons salsa

cilantro for garnish

1. Preheat oven to 400 degrees. Line a 10×13-inch pan with aluminum foil. Spread a tablespoon of oil evenly over the foil.

2. Place the fillets on the prepared pan.

3. In a small bowl, combine the garlic powder, salt, lemon pepper, and Italian seasoning. Sprinkle the seasoning mixture over the fillets.

4. Cover the fillets with aluminum foil. Bake for 12 minutes.

5. Garnish the fillets with the salsa and cilantro before serving.

Snapper Florentine

 SONG PAIRING: "Sailing" composed and sung by Christopher Cross.

Yield: 4–6 servings

Serving Suggestion: Serve the fish with rice or pasta.

INGREDIENTS
¼ cup butter or canola oil
1½ cups spinach
1 lemon
5–6 snapper filets
1 teaspoon salt
1 teaspoon ground black pepper
2 tablespoons garlic powder
2 tablespoons lemon pepper

I was born in Jacksonville, Florida where snapper is a local favorite. Make this dish to find out why. The taste and consistency can't be beat!

1. Preheat the oven to 375 degrees. Grease a baking pan with butter. Make a spinach bed in the pan for each snapper fillet.

2. Cut the lemon in half. Squeeze the juice from half of the lemon sections over the spinach. Place the snapper on the spinach beds.

3. Squeeze the remaining lemon half on the snapper. Sprinkle the salt, ground black pepper, garlic powder, and lemon pepper on the fish.

4. Cover the pan with aluminum foil. Cook for 20 minutes.

Grilled Snapper

 SONG PAIRING: "Sweet Home Alabama" by Lynyrd Skynyrd.

Yield: 2–3 servings

INGREDIENTS

½ cup olive oil

3–4 snapper filets

1 teaspoon salt

1 tablespoon ground black pepper

¼ cup lime juice

1. Preheat the grill. When hot, place a sheet of aluminum foil on the grill grates to keep the fish from falling through.

2. Spread olive oil over the foil to prevent sticking.

3. Put the fish on the aluminum foil. Cook the fish for 3 minutes on each side.

4. Top the fish with salt, ground black pepper, and lime juice.

This recipe takes no time and it will get everyone to the dinner table!

Using mesquite or other woodchips on your grill will increase the flavor.

Poached Salmon

 SONG PAIRING: "The Wreck of the Edmond Fitzgerald."
Gordon Lightfoot sang this one.

Yield: 3–4 servings

Serving Suggestion: Serve the salmon with ranch dressing, dill sauce, or sour cream on the side. Garnish for color with fruits like blueberries, raspberries, and strawberries, or vegetable slices like carrots, scallions or peppers.

This fish is the "I want another piece" fish! Hot or cold, baked, broiled, or grilled, it doesn't matter. Salmon is king and always will be!

INGREDIENTS
1 cup white wine
2 bay leaves
1 teaspoon oregano leaves
1 teaspoon sage
2 tablespoons olive oil
3–4 medium salmon fillets
bib lettuce or leaf lettuce, for garnish

1. In a large pot combine the white wine, bay leaves, oregano, sage, and olive oil. Bring to a boil over high heat.

2. Reduce the heat to medium low. Put the salmon in the pot. Cover the pot. Let simmer for 8 to 10 minutes. Carefully remove the salmon from the pot.

3. Arrange the lettuce in a bed on a serving plate. Lay the salmon on top.

Asian Salmon

 SONG PAIRING: "Something Wonderful" from *The King and I.*

Yield: 3–5 servings

Serving Suggestion: Serve the salmon over white or brown rice.

INGREDIENTS

¼ cup olive oil

¼ cup butter

4 tablespoons sesame oil

1/8 cup red or white wine

2 tablespoons garlic powder

2 tablespoons ginger

1 lime, juiced

1/8 cup soy sauce

1/8 cup teriyaki sauce

3–4 medium salmon fillets

1. In a sauté pan, combine the olive oil, butter, sesame oil, wine, garlic powder, ginger, and lime juice. Bring the ingredients to a simmer over medium heat.

2. Stir the soy and teriyaki sauce. Add the salmon fillets.

3. Cook the salmon in the sauce over medium heat for 6 to 8 minutes. Spoon any remaining sauce over each salmon fillet before serving.

Italian Salmon

 SONG PAIRING: "Maria" from *West Side Story.*

Yield: 4–6 servings

Here is a very easy, simple way to make salmon in less than 15 minutes.

INGREDIENTS
1 pound penne rigate or any pasta of
   your choice
¼ cup olive oil
¼ cup butter or parve margarine
3 cloves garlic, diced
¼ cup white wine
4 tablespoons fresh dill, diced
4–6 (8 ounce) salmon filets or 2–3
   pounds of salmon
¼ cup Italian dressing
1 cup Italian parsley
1 lemon, sliced

1. Fill a pot with water and bring to a boil. Cook pasta according to directions
   on the box. Drain pasta in a colander and set aside.

2. In a sauté pan, combine olive oil, butter, and garlic. Simmer the ingredients
   for 1 minute over medium heat.

3. Stir in the white wine and dill. Add the salmon fillets. Simmer over medium
   heat for 3 minutes.

4. Add the Italian dressing to the pan. Simmer ingredients for 2 minutes.

5. Remove the salmon. Serve the fish over the pasta. Spoon the sauce from
   the pan over the salmon and pasta. Garnish with Italian parsley and sliced
   lemon.

Pan Fried Walleye

 SONG PAIRING: "Young at Heart" by Frank Sinatra.

Yield: 4–6 servings

Serving Suggestion: Serve with vegetables or rice.

This is one of my favorite recipes and a Minnesota favorite. Try substituting saltines for finely crushed Corn Flakes. Both ways will knock your socks off!

INGREDIENTS
6 eggs
6–8 cups crushed saltines or cornflakes
1 teaspoon salt
1 teaspoon ground black pepper
2 cups flour
6 walleye fillets
2 cups canola oil
chopped walnuts for garnish (optional)

1. Scramble the eggs in one bowl. Put the saltines in a second bowl. Put the salt, pepper, and flour in a third bowl.

2. Dip both sides of a fillet in the flour mixture. Dip both sides of the fillet in the egg mixture. Dip both sides of the fillet in the saltines.

3. In a sauté pan, heat canola oil over high heat. When hot, carefully place the prepared fish in the pan. The fish should crackle and sizzle. Brown the fish on both sides for 2 to 3 minutes.

4. Place the walleye on paper towels to absorb any extra oil before serving.

QUICHE

Quiche is not traditionally a Jewish food. In fact, although it is a French cuisine classic, quiche has many Germanic influences. It originated on the border of France and Germany in the Alsace-Lorrain region. The word "quiche" is derived from the German word "kuchen," which means cake. I gave this delicious "cake" it's own section because it is an adaptable kosher classic.

The variations I have made over the years make each quiche unique. When I was growing up Bubbie would make a great Jewish meal of lox, eggs, and onions. Zaddie and I couldn't get enough! When I began cooking professionally, I perfected a recipe for lox and sour cream quiche. Every kosher eater I have ever met loves this quiche, even though it is nontraditional. Check it out. But don't stop there!

For breakfast, compliment quiche with fruit. At lunch, offer it with a side salad. Serve it at dinner next to any rice and top with nuts. You just can't go wrong with quiche. All of the quiches in this section will get rave reviews at any time of day!

Cheese Quiche

 SONG PAIRING: "Good Day Sunshine" by The Beatles.

Yield: two 9-inch pies

Serving Suggestion: Substitute any of the following cheeses for the Swiss cheese: cheddar, Colby, herb spread, Havarti, mozzarella, or smoked Gouda.

This is the basic recipe for all my quiches. It only takes 30 minutes to make. Use your favorite cheese!

To keep within the laws of Kashrut check the ingredient list on food items you purchase and look for the symbol "U" for Kosher. There are stores in most areas that sell piecrusts without lard.

INGREDIENTS

10 eggs

2 cups half and half

2 cups sour cream

1 teaspoon salt

1 teaspoon ground black pepper

2 cups shredded Swiss cheese, or any cheese you like

2 premade piecrusts

1. Preheat the oven to 350 degrees.

2. Crack the eggs into a bowl. Add the half and half, sour cream, salt and ground black pepper. Whisk aggressively until the mixture is uniform and has a small froth. The froth is a sign of oxidation and that the ingredients are well mixed.

3. Fill each piecrust to half full with the egg mixture. Add the cheese to the piecrusts, dividing it evenly. Divide the remaining egg mixture between the two piecrusts.

4. Bake both quiches for 20 to 25 minutes. Check every 10 minutes. The quiche is done when the top rises a bit over the pie shell, like a small dome. Let cool for 5 to 7 minutes before cutting.

Israeli Quiche

  SONG PAIRING: "Hava Nagila!" or "Artza Alinu."

Yield: two 9-inch pies

INGREDIENTS

2 tablespoons butter

1 red pepper, chopped

1 large zucchini, chopped

2 premade piecrusts

2 cups grated Havarti cheese

10 eggs

2 cups half and half

2 cups sour cream

1 tablespoon garlic powder

2 tablespoons cumin

1 tablespoon thyme

¼ teaspoon salt

¼ teaspoon ground black pepper

1. Preheat the oven to 350 degrees. In a sauté pan, melt butter over high heat. Add the pepper and zucchini to the pan. Cook for 2 minutes.

2. Put the cooked vegetables in the piecrusts, dividing equally between the two piecrusts. Add the cheese to the piecrusts, dividing it evenly.

3. Crack the eggs into a bowl. Add the half and half, sour cream, garlic powder, cumin, and thyme to the bowl. Whisk aggressively until the mixture is uniform and has a small froth. The froth is a sign of oxidation and that the ingredients are well mixed. Add the salt and pepper to the bowl.

4. Fill each piecrust to half full with the egg mixture. Evenly spread the ingredients in each piecrust. Divide the remaining egg mixture between the two piecrusts.

5. Bake both quiches for 20 to 25 minutes. Check every 10 minutes. The quiche is done when the top rises a bit over the pie shell, like a small dome. Let cool for 5 to 7 minutes before cutting.

Broccoli and Cheese Quiche

 SONG PAIRING: "Here Comes the Sun" by George Harrison.

Yield: two 9-inch pies

INGREDIENTS

2 cups chopped broccoli

2 premade piecrusts

2 cups grated Swiss cheese

10 eggs

2 cups half and half

2 cups sour cream

1 tablespoon garlic powder

4 teaspoons oregano

¼ teaspoon salt

¼ teaspoon ground black pepper

1. Preheat the oven to 350 degrees. Put the broccoli and ½ cup water in a loosely covered microwave safe container. Microwave for 2 minutes on high. Drain the liquid from the broccoli.

2. Put the cooked broccoli in the piecrusts, dividing equally between the two piecrusts. Add the cheese to the piecrusts, dividing it evenly.

3. Crack the eggs into a bowl. Add the half and half, sour cream, garlic powder, and oregano to the bowl. Whisk aggressively until the mixture is uniform and has a small froth. The froth is a sign of oxidation and that the ingredients are well mixed. Add the salt and pepper to the bowl.

4. Fill each piecrust to half full with the egg mixture. Evenly spread the ingredients in each piecrust. Divide the remaining egg mixture between the two piecrusts.

5. Bake for 20 to 25 minutes. Check every 10 minutes. The quiche is done when the top rises a bit over the pie shell, like a small dome. Let cool for 5 to 7 minutes before cutting.

Spinach and Mushroom Quiche

 SONG PAIRING: Theme song from the cartoon *Popeye the Sailor Man.*

Yield: two 9-inch pies

INGREDIENTS

2 tablespoons butter
   or 3 tablespoons olive oil
4 cups fresh spinach
2 cups sliced mushrooms
2 premade piecrusts
2 cups shredded mozzarella cheese
10 eggs

2 cups half and half
2 cups sour cream
1 tablespoon garlic powder
2 tablespoons basil
¼ teaspoon salt
¼ teaspoon ground black pepper

1. Preheat the oven to 350 degrees. In a sauté pan, melt butter over high heat. Stir in the spinach and mushrooms. Cook for 1½ to 2 minutes.

2. Put the spinach and mushrooms in the piecrusts, dividing equally between the two piecrusts. Add the cheese to the piecrusts, dividing it evenly.

3. Crack the eggs into a bowl. Add the half and half, sour cream, garlic powder, and basil. Whisk aggressively until the mixture is uniform with a small froth. The froth is a sign of oxidation and that the ingredients are well mixed. Add the salt and pepper to the bowl.

4. Fill each piecrust to half full with the egg mixture. Evenly spread the ingredients in each piecrust. Divide the remaining egg mixture between the two piecrusts.

> I'm a spinach guy. Cooked or raw, spinach is my thing! When I was a kid in the school lunchroom I would trade desserts for spinach! I thought that the more spinach I ate the bigger my muscles would get. Maybe it was from watching too many Popeye cartoons, but it seemed to work. This quiche might prove there is a little Popeye in you too.

5. Bake for 20 to 25 minutes. Check every 10 minutes. The quiche is done when the top rises a bit over the pie shell, like a small dome. Let cool for 5 to 7 minutes before cutting.

Lox and Sour Cream Quiche

Yield: two 9-inch pies

INGREDIENTS

2 tablespoons butter or
   3 tablespoons olive oil
2 cups thin sliced lox
1 cup diced scallions
2 premade parve piecrusts
10 eggs

2 cups half and half
2 cups sour cream
1 tablespoon garlic powder
2 tablespoons basil
¼ teaspoon salt
¼ teaspoon ground black pepper

1. Preheat the oven to 350 degrees.

2. Divide the lox and scallions equally between the two piecrusts.

3. Crack the eggs into a bowl. Add the half and half, sour cream, garlic powder, and basil. Whisk aggressively until the mixture is uniform with a small froth. The froth is a sign of oxidation and that the ingredients are well mixed. Add the salt and pepper to the bowl.

4. Fill each piecrust to half full with the egg mixture. Evenly spread the ingredients in each piecrust. Divide the remaining egg mixture between the two piecrusts.

5. Bake for 20 to 25 minutes. Check every 10 minutes. The quiche is done when the top rises a bit over the pie shell, like a small dome. Let cool for 5 to 7 minutes before cutting.

VEGETABLES

When I was a child I was a big proponent of vegetables. Really! Carrots, peppers, celery, and zucchini—I loved them all. Some people are not so hot on vegetables, but I have a remedy for that. This section has vegetable recipes you can serve to anyone you know. All you have to do is get them to eat one bite!

One of my favorite vegetable success stories comes from my own family. When my children were young, I had a simple recipe to get them to eat the one vegetable many kids hate, broccoli. I cooked broccoli florets al dente and topped them with a little marmalade sauce. As time went on I graduated to adding flavor on the side, using dips like dill or ranch dressing. To this day my kids don't know why they like the taste broccoli, they just do.

For kosher vegetarian meals use Alfredo sauce. For kosher fleishig meals use parve margarine and garlic, or parve hollandaise sauce.

Vegetables are an easy side or main dish to prepare that's kosher. Whether you are a young parent or young adult just learning how to cook, vegetables make the perfect side dish for any meal. My recipes also encourage creativity. Vegetables can be steamed, sautéed, boiled, grilled, or roasted. They can be complemented with a light sauce or served plain. Let your imagination run wild. With vegetables, there are no limitations. So, which vegetable recipe are YOU making tonight?

Simple Cooked Vegetables

Yield: 4–6 servings

If you feel like a little something sweet, try a little bit of apricot or orange marmalade sauce on the top of my cooked vegetables. Just mix 1¼ cup hot water and 2 tablespoons marmalade in a bowl. Blend together to create a sauce. It tastes yummy!

Prepare the vegetables you plan to use before cooking. Cut the large ends off the asparagus. Chop broccoli into florets. Cut the ends off the Brussels sprouts. Then cut them in half. Thinly slice any mushrooms, squash, or zucchini.

INGREDIENTS

3–6 cups assorted vegetables
½ cup parve margarine or butter
1 teaspoon garlic powder

1 teaspoon salt, pepper, garlic,
  or dill, to taste
1 cup light sauce, see box or the sauce
  section for ideas (optional)

Sauté the vegetables:

1. In a sauté pan, combine the vegetables with parve margarine and garlic powder. Sauté over medium high heat for 2 to 3 minutes. When sautéing, be sure not to overcook the vegetables. The vegetables should remain firm.

2. Pour the sauce over the vegetables just before serving.

Steam the vegetables:

1. Microwave the vegetables in a microwave safe container with ½ cup water for approximately 2½ minutes on high.

2. Let the vegetables sit for 1 to 2 minutes. Drain the water. Stir in the salt, pepper, garlic, or dill to taste. Pour the sauce over the vegetables before serving.

Eggplant Parmigianino

Yield: 3–4 servings

Some people love eggplant. Some people avoid it at all costs. I've found that this recipe works really well for the non-eggplant eaters in my family.

INGREDIENTS

1 cup grated Parmesan

2 cups grated mozzarella cheese

2 tablespoons butter

2 cups chopped onions

1 teaspoon salt

1 teaspoon oregano

3 teaspoons cornstarch

1 tablespoon garlic powder

1 (16 ounce) can diced tomatoes

5–6 cups diced eggplant

3 slices dry bread, crumbled

Nonstick spray (optional)

1. Preheat the oven to 350 degrees. Grease a 9×12-inch pan. In a bowl, combine Parmesan and mozzarella.

2. In a sauté pan, melt butter over high heat. Stir in the onions, salt, oregano, cornstarch, and garlic powder. Simmer the ingredients for 2 minutes. Put the ingredients into a large bowl.

3. Put the tomatoes, eggplant, and bread into the bowl. Add half of the cheese mixture to the bowl, saving the other half of the mixture for the top. Stir the mixture lightly.

4. Pour the mixture into the pan. Top with remaining cheese. Bake for 40 to 45 minutes.

Mediterranean Eggplant

 SONG PAIRING: "Shall We Dance?" from *The King and I*.

Yield: 4–6 servings

INGREDIENTS

½ cup olive oil

1 large eggplant, cut into strips

4 scallions, chopped

2 tablespoons soy sauce

1½ teaspoons white sugar

1 teaspoon ground ginger

1 teaspoon salt

½ teaspoon hot pepper sauce

2 tablespoons parsley, chopped

1. In a skillet warm the olive oil over medium high heat. When the oil is hot add the eggplant. Cook until slightly browned. Stir the mixture occasionally.

2. Stir in the scallions, soy sauce, white sugar, ginger, salt, hot pepper sauce, and ¼ cup water. Sprinkle on 1 tablespoon of the parsley.

3. Simmer over medium heat for 30 minutes, stirring occasionally.

4. Before serving, sprinkle the remaining parsley over the top.

One day while pressed for time I wanted to get dinner in the oven before I had to leave for a meeting. I looked in the refrigerator and noticed I had ricotta cheese. It started me thinking ... do I have shredded cheese, vegetables, and marinara sauce for lasagna? How about lasagna noodles? To my surprise, I had a little bit of everything! The only thing I didn't have was the time to cook lasagna. I thought to myself, "Well, I know that the noodles are supposed to be cooked before they are baked, but what will happen if I don't cook them all the way first?" I put the noodles in hot water while I got dressed. I quickly chopped mushrooms, zucchini, and fresh spinach. I layered the noodles with cheese, vegetables, and marinara sauce in a pan. I put a little cheese on the top, covered it with aluminum foil, and stuck it in the heated oven. I was ready to go to my meeting!

When I arrived home an hour and twenty minutes later my kids said, "We're starving. What smells so good?" I told them, "I've tried an experiment, let's see how it tastes." To my surprise, the lasagna was incredible! And it took only a little over ten minutes to put together. I said to my kids, "If I ever write a cookbook, I'm going to put this one in!"

To this day, even when I'm not pressed for time, this is how I make lasagna. Put in whatever ingredients appeal to you. This is something you can make in a hurry and come back to compliments! You never know what you can do until you don't have time.

Cantor's Quick Vegetable Lasagna

 SONG PAIRING: "As Time Goes By" from the movie *Casablanca*.

Yield: 4–6 servings

INGREDIENTS

1 pound lasagna noodles

1 pint container ricotta cheese

4–6 cups shredded cheese of your choice

1 cup sliced mushrooms

1 large zucchini, sliced

4 cups spinach

1 (24 ounce) jar marinara
   or spaghetti sauce

1. Preheat the oven to 350 degrees. Soak the noodles in hot water for 3 minutes.

2. In a 9×12-inch pan, layer the noodles, ricotta, 3 cups shredded cheese, vegetables, spinach. Fill to near the top of the pan.

3. Sprinkle the remaining shredded cheese over the top.

4. Cover the pan with aluminum foil. Bake for 80 minutes.

Teriyaki String Beans

 SONG PAIRING: "It's a Puzzlement" from *The King and I.*

Yield: 3–4 servings

Serving Suggestion: This has become my signature vegetable dish. It compliments any entrée perfectly!

My family loves this recipe and so will yours!

INGREDIENTS
1 pound fresh green string beans
1 cup parve margarine or butter
1 (8 ounce) can water chestnuts or bamboo shoots, drained
4 tablespoons teriyaki sauce
4 tablespoons soy sauce
½ lime, juiced

1. Cut off the ends of the beans.

2. In a sauté pan, melt the butter over medium high heat. Stir in the beans and water chestnuts. Sauté the beans for 2 minutes, stir or flip the string beans frequently. Add the teriyaki sauce and soy sauce to the pan.

3. Sauté beans in the sauce for 1 to 2 minutes. Taste the beans to judge if they are sufficiently cooked. The beans should still have a bit of a crunch. Once the beans have the desired consistency, add the lime juice. Sauté over high heat for an additional minute.

SAUCES

Everyone wants to make simple recipes. It is so easy to go to the store and buy a red sauce, Alfredo sauce, or pesto sauce. They make your meal preparation quick. Sometimes, when life gets hectic, that's just what you need. So why bother to make a sauce from scratch? The answer is simple: creativity!

In this section, creativity abounds. For me, spirituality equals creativity. There is something spiritual I find when making a sauce and using it to complete a dish. It is the finishing touch on a special meal, an additional flavor, and it always enhances the dish. There are those of you who want to stretch out your cooking skills—this section is for you.

I first learned to make sauces while working as a sous chef in New York City. It increased my ability to match the right sauce with the right food through experimentation. I developed these recipes and tested each one on my family with rave reviews. I believe each sauce makes a great match for many meals. These recipes are really easy too. Your family and friends will love the added flavor, and they will be amazed with your cooking prowess.

Remember if you are using your sauce with a fleishig dish, parve margarine will keep it kosher. If you are using your sauce with vegetables or fish, choose butter.

Garlic Herb Sauce

Yield: 3–4 servings

Serving Suggestion: This sauce goes great with any chicken dish or grilled fish!

INGREDIENTS

1 cup parve margarine, or butter

2 tablespoons minced garlic

½ teaspoon thyme

½ teaspoon oregano

½ teaspoon basil

2 tablespoons lemon juice

1 teaspoon cornstarch

salt and ground black pepper (optional)

1. In a sauté pan, melt the parve margarine over medium heat. Stir in the garlic. Sauté the mixture for 1 minute.

2. Stir in the thyme, oregano, basil, lemon juice, and cornstarch. Whisk the ingredients over medium heat until the sauce thickens, about 1 to 2 minutes.

3. Season with salt and pepper. Taste and adjust the seasoning before serving.

Garnish any dish you use this sauce on with cut artichoke hearts, capers, or diced mango.

Winning Wine Sauce

Yield: 3–4 servings

Serving Suggestion: This is a great sauce to use over chicken or fish.

INGREDIENTS
1 cup parve margarine or butter
¼ cup red wine or white wine
1 bay leaf
1 teaspoon salt
1 teaspoon ground black pepper
½ teaspoon garlic powder
1 teaspoon flour, plus extra for thickening
salt (optional)

1. In a sauté pan, combine all the ingredients over medium heat. Whisk the ingredients vigorously for 1 minute.

2. For a thicker sauce add a bit of flour and water mixed together. Whisk vigorously.

3. Season with salt. Taste and adjust the seasoning before serving.

White Sauce

Yield: 3–4 servings

Serving Suggestion: This sauce can be used over pasta or fish.

INGREDIENTS

3 tablespoons butter

2 teaspoons flour, plus extra
  for thickening

1 cup milk

1 tablespoon Herbs de Provence

½ tablespoon onion powder

½ teaspoon nutmeg

1. In a sauté pan, melt the butter over medium heat. Whisk in the flour and water mixture. The flour and butter will thicken to create a roux.

2. Slowly add the milk, Herbs de Provence, onion powder, and nutmeg. Whisk the roux until the sauce is smooth.

3. For a thicker sauce add a pinch of flour at a time. Whisk vigorously.

4. Season with salt and pepper. Taste and adjust the seasoning before serving.

Dijon Mustard Sauce

Yield: 3–4 servings

Serving Suggestion: This is a great sauce to use over meat. Substitute butter for the parve margarine if you plan to serve this sauce with fish.

INGREDIENTS
1 cup parve margarine or butter
2 tablespoons Dijon mustard
1 teaspoon garlic powder
1 teaspoon lemon pepper
1 teaspoon fresh dill
salt and pepper (optional)

1. Put all the ingredients in a bowl. Whisk vigorously until ingredients are combined.

2. Season with salt and pepper if desired. Taste and adjust the seasoning before serving.

Hollandaise Sauce

Yield: 3–4 servings

Serving Suggestion: Compliments chicken, fish, and vegetables.

INGREDIENTS

4 egg yolks

4 teaspoons lemon juice

½ teaspoon salt

½ teaspoon garlic powder

7 tablespoons parve margarine or butter

¼ teaspoon cayenne pepper (optional)

¼ teaspoon ground nutmeg (optional)

1. In a bowl, combine the egg yolks, lemon juice, salt, garlic powder, and 5 tablespoons cold water. Whisk the ingredients together.

2. In a sauté pan, melt parve margarine over low heat. Slowly stir in the egg mixture. Continue stirring the sauce until it thickens.

3. Add the cayenne pepper or nutmeg for extra flavor.

SALADS

Don't let salad become a boring diet food in your house. I eat salad at least three times a week and love every bite! How do I do it? By keeping it fresh. I change dressings from spicy to mild. I use different vegetables every time to get different type of crunch. Or I try adding an avocado to add a smooth texture.

Salad prep is fun for me too. Why? Because of all the chopping, dicing, and slicing. In fact, you can develop your knife skills by making more salads. At dinner parties I demonstrate how to cut vegetables while blindfolded. I'm not suggesting you try this, but you should never be intimidated by the chopping it takes to make a salad.

Salads can round out a meal or become a great snack. If made correctly, they treat your taste buds to an explosion of flavors and textures. Even better, most salads are an easy and delicious all kosher dish. So get your vegetables out of the refrigerator and start chopping! Let your imagination run wild!

Herb Salad

Yield: 4–6 servings

INGREDIENTS
4 cups lettuce or mixed greens
2 medium tomatoes, sliced
1 large cucumber, sliced
¼ cup chopped chives
¼ cup red onion, sliced
½ cup croutons
¼ cup Italian dressing

1. Combine all of the ingredients in a large bowl.

2. Toss the ingredients to mix.

3. Chill for 30 minutes. Toss again before serving.

Spinach Salad

Yield: 4–6 servings

INGREDIENTS

4 cups fresh spinach

1 cup sliced strawberries

¼ cup caramelized pecans

½ red onion, thin sliced

1 red pepper, thin sliced

¼ cup balsamic vinaigrette

¼ cup olive oil

1 teaspoon white sugar (optional)

1. Combine all of the ingredients in a large bowl, or build ingredients on serving plates.

2. Toss the ingredients to mix.

3. Chill for 30 minutes. Toss again before serving.

Niçoise Salad

Yield: 4–6 servings

INGREDIENTS

6 small red or golden potatoes, cooked
2 cups fresh green beans, blanched
½ cup black olives, sliced
2 tomatoes, thinly sliced
½ red onion, thinly sliced
1 (12 ounce) canned tuna, drained
2 hard-boiled eggs, quartered
4–6 large leaves romaine lettuce
French or Italian dressing

1. Combine the potatoes, green beans, olives, tomatoes, red onions, tuna, and eggs in a large bowl.

2. Toss the ingredients to mix. Chill the mixture for 20 minutes.

3. Make a bed of the lettuce on a serving plate. Serve the chilled mixture over the lettuce.

Avocado and Fruit Salad

Yield: 4–6 servings

INGREDIENTS
¼ cup hot water
½ cup honey
1 teaspoon nutmeg
¼ cup lemon or orange zest
2 apples, cored and sliced
2 oranges
2 cups grapes, halved
1 cup blueberries or strawberries
1 avocado, peeled and sliced

1. Combine the water, honey, nutmeg, and lemon zest together in a large bowl to make a honey dressing. Set aside.

2. Combine the apples, oranges, grapes, blueberries, and avocado together in another bowl. Chill the fruit mixture for 15 minutes.

3. Pour the honey dressing over the fruit mixture before serving.

Chicken Salad

Yield: 4–6 servings

Serving Suggestion: Serve on a bed of greens or build a terrific sandwich.

INGREDIENTS

3 cooked kosher chicken breasts, chopped

2 hard boiled eggs, chopped

2 tablespoons lemon juice

1 (8 ounce) can water chestnuts, drained and chopped

1 (3 ounce) bottle onion flakes

½ cup cashews

1 cup mayonnaise

1 cup diced celery

salt and ground black pepper, to taste

1. Combine all the ingredients in a large bowl. Season with salt and pepper. Toss to mix.

2. Chill for at least several hours, up to a day before serving.

Ambrosia Salad

Love this sweet salad!

Yield: 4–6 servings

INGREDIENTS

1 (3 ounce) package orange gelatin
½ cup white sugar
3 oranges, peeled and cut into
   bite sized pieces

1 (8 ounce) can crushed pineapple
1 cup flaked coconut
1 cup chopped pecans
1 (8 ounce) container sour cream

1. In a medium mixing bowl, dissolve the gelatin and white sugar in 1 cup boiling water.

2. Chill the mixture until it begins to thicken, about 5 to 10 minutes.

3. Add the remaining ingredients to the bowl. Stir to mix the ingredients together.

4. Pour the mixture into a 9×13-inch pan. Chill until firm or about 45 minutes. Cut the salad into squares before serving.

PIES

What do you think of when you think of an all-American food? I think of pie. Pie rounds off every great family meal. At holiday time, going out to eat, or at a family reunion, a slice of pie is a slice of America.

I first started making pies as a prep chef in New York. The daily menu featured two pies: one fruit pie and one mystery pie. The best selling mystery pie was always the French Silk Pie, or it was—until I introduced my version of Southern Pecan Pie. You can find the recipe for that one in this section.

Every pie in this section is easy to prepare. So why not give it a shot? One thing is for sure; nearly everyone has a sweet tooth. The pies in this book will satisfy your sweet tooth every time. It's bound to please everyone else at the table too!

Keep things simple. The hardest part of a pie is the crust. Instead of making the crust, buy it. Many stores sell a variety of pie shells that contain no lard. Check the ingredients to be sure that they are kosher. You can also make or purchase graham cracker crusts to serve with a milchig meal.

Peach Pie

Yield: 4–6 servings

Serving Suggestion: If serving after a milk meal top with vanilla ice cream and/or whipped cream.

INGREDIENTS

2 cups peaches, peeled or unpeeled
   and sliced
1 premade piecrust
2 eggs

2 tablespoons flour
1 cup white sugar
¼ cup butter, melted

1. Preheat the oven to 400 degrees. Put the peaches in the piecrust. Spread them evenly over the crust.

2. In a bowl, combine the eggs, flour, white sugar, and butter. Pour the mixture over the peaches.

3. Place a baking sheet under the pie to catch any juices that may boil over the top! Bake the pie for 15 minutes. Reduce the heat to 300 degrees. Bake for an additional 50 minutes. Check the pie frequently.

Pear Pie

Yield: 4–6 servings

Serving Suggestion: If serving after a milk meal top with vanilla ice cream and/or whipped cream.

INGREDIENTS

2 cups sliced pears

1 premade piecrust

2 eggs

2 tablespoons flour

1 cup white sugar

¼ cup butter, melted

1. Preheat the oven to 400 degrees. Put the pears in the piecrust. Spread them evenly over the crust.

2. In a bowl, combine the eggs, flour, white sugar, and butter. Pour the mixture over the pears.

3. Place a baking sheet under the pie to catch any juices that may boil over the top!

4. Bake the pie for 15 minutes. Reduce the heat to 300 degrees. Bake for an additional 50 minutes. Check the pie frequently.

Key Lime Pie

Yield: 4–6 servings

Serving Suggestion: Serve this pie as a milk meal dessert. Try a slice as a snack with coffee. Garnish with whipped cream and a curl of lime rind, a small wedge of lime or even a strawberry!

INGREDIENTS

1 (14 ounce) can sweetened
  condensed milk
1 tablespoon grated key lime rind
½ cup key lime juice
¼ teaspoon salt

3 egg yolks, beaten
1 premade piecrust
3 egg whites
2 tablespoons white sugar

1. Preheat the oven to 350 degrees. Put the condensed milk, key lime rind, key lime juice, salt, and egg yolks in a bowl. Stir until the mixture becomes thick. Pour the mixture into the piecrust.

2. Beat the egg whites in a bowl until just combined. Add the white sugar to the bowl. Whisk or beat the mixture until it is stiff.

3. Spoon the egg white mixture over the top of the pie filling. Bake for 10 to 15 minutes. Let cool for 20 minutes.

Pecan Pie

Yield: 4–6 servings

Serving Suggestion: Substitute parve margarine for butter to serve this pie as a dessert for a meat meal. Garnish with whipped cream and a mint leaf if you are serving the pie after a milk meal.

INGREDIENTS

3 eggs
1 cup white sugar
½ teaspoon salt
¼ cup butter or parve margarine
1 cup corn syrup
1 cup pecan halves
1 tablespoon vanilla
1 premade piecrust

1. Preheat the oven to 350 degrees.

2. In a bowl, whisk the eggs, white sugar, salt, butter, and corn syrup. Stir in the pecan halves and vanilla. Pour the mixture into the piecrust.

3. Bake for 40 to 50 minutes. Let the pie cool for 10 minutes if serving warm. Put the pie in the refrigerator for 10 minutes to serve cold.

French Silk Pie

Yield: 4–6 servings

Serving Suggestion: Substitute parve margarine for butter to serve this pie as a dessert after a meat meal. Garnish the pie with raspberries, blueberries, and chopped nuts. Try topping with whipped cream if serving the pie after a milk meal.

INGREDIENTS
2 ounces unsweetened chocolate
½ cup butter or parve margarine, softened
¾ cup white sugar
2 teaspoons confectioners' white sugar
1 teaspoon vanilla
2 eggs
1 premade piecrust

1. Microwave the chocolate in a small bowl for 15 seconds. Stir the chocolate. Continue microwaving in 15-second intervals until the chocolate is melted.

2. Put the butter in a mixing bowl. Gradually stir in the white sugar and confectioners' white sugar until the ingredients well blended. Add the chocolate and vanilla to the bowl, beating to combine ingredients. Add one egg at a time to the bowl, beating for 2 minutes after each egg. Spoon the chocolate filling into the piecrust.

3. Refrigerate for 2 to 3 hours before serving.

SORBETS

Sorbets are light non-filling desserts that are just plain fun. In the kosher cookbooks I have read, sorbets are hardly ever included as a great kosher option. This is a shame. Sorbets are my number one kosher dessert for a new generation! They are so simple. The machine does all the work. Even better, it is a great dessert with so many variations.

I discovered sorbets while shopping for a new sauté pan. I noticed all the food prep machines in the store. Of course, one machine caught my eye right away. It was an ice cream and sorbet maker. Thus began my adventure in making sorbets out of juices, fruits, milk, coffee, and chocolate. You name it; I've tried to make a sorbet out of it. Frankly, my family has had more sorbets in the last four months than the average person has in a lifetime!

Since my purchase of the sorbet maker my family and friends have voted me the reigning sorbet king. As king I've got to be generous. I'm going to give you all the favorite recipes. Buy your own machine. See what you can create. Don't forget to call me. I'll be right over to taste!

To achieve the best consistency, put the finished product in serving glasses, and freeze for 5 to 10 minutes before serving. The sorbet will hold longer, and the texture will be silky smooth.

For a milk meal, substitute 1½ cup of any juice with 1½ cup half and half. It makes a creamy and delicious sorbet.

Add a little kick! Pour in two shots of Baileys, Frangelico Liqueur, or Grand Mariner to the mix. The liqueur and fruit work well together.

You can adjust the white sugar in each sorbet by a tablespoon. You can also replace the white sugar with an artificial sweetener. Any way you make it, a sorbet is a wonderful finish to any meal.

Strawberry Sorbet

Yield: 3–4 servings

INGREDIENTS

4 cups fresh or frozen strawberries
1 cup pineapple juice
1 tablespoon white sugar
1 tablespoon almond extract

1. Put the strawberries in a blender or food processor. Blend until smooth.

2. Combine the strawberries, pineapple juice, white sugar, almond extract, and ½ cup water in a bowl. Pour into the sorbet machine container. Start and run for approximately 10 minutes or desired thickness.

Orange Sorbet

Yield: 3–4 servings

INGREDIENTS
4 cups orange juice
4 tablespoons white sugar
1 tablespoon vanilla extract

1. Combine the ingredients in a bowl. Pour into the sorbet machine container.

2. Freeze according the manufacturer's instructions or desired thickness.

Guava Sorbet

Yield: 3–4 servings

INGREDIENTS
4 cups guava juice
4 tablespoons white sugar
1 tablespoon hazelnut extract

1. Combine the ingredients in a bowl. Pour into the sorbet machine container.

2. Freeze according the manufacturer's instructions or desired thickness.

Mango Sorbet

Yield: 3–4 servings

INGREDIENTS
4 cups mango juice
4 tablespoons white sugar

1. Combine the ingredients in a bowl. Pour into the sorbet machine container.

2. Freeze according the manufacturer's instructions or desired thickness.

Chai Tea Sorbet

Yield: 3–4 servings

INGREDIENTS

½ cup coffee

½ cup chai tea concentrate

3 cups milk

2 tablespoons white sugar

1. Combine the ingredients in a bowl.
   Pour into the sorbet machine container.

2. Freeze according the manufacturer's instructions or desired thickness.

Pineapple & Coconut Sorbet

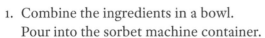

Yield: 3–4 servings

INGREDIENTS

1 cup pineapple

2 cups coconut

4 tablespoons white sugar

1 tablespoon almond extract

1. Combine the ingredients in a bowl.
   Pour into the sorbet machine container.

2. Freeze according the manufacturer's instructions
   or dcsired thickness.

BUBBIE THE BAKER
SWEET BREADS AND DESSERTS

There are not enough words to express my gratitude and love for my mom, Bubbie Marie. As a cook and baker there is no one better! During my time in New York City she would often send me baked goods. My favorite was the banana bread. After a visit to my parents I noticed the banana bread tasted different at home. Now, the banana bread at home was fabulous, but the banana bread in New York was fantastic! When I squeezed a slice to put it in my mouth it seemed to ooze with flavor.

Back then I was stumped. I thought all baked goods would taste basically the same. Today, I think being far from home may have had something to do with it! Even now when I make banana bread I let it sit for a few days. It helps me remember how lucky I am to have such an incredible mom who loves baking for her son.

I never thought I could do justice to mom's baking, but I found that her recipes are foolproof, even for a schlemiel like me! I want to share them with you. This part of the book is filled with her Jewishness, love, and yiddishkeit! Baking her recipes will bring you back to a time when life was simpler. Like Bubbie, you can make your home a place where the heart is and where the baked goods should be!

Blonde Brownies

Yield: 16 servings

Serving Suggestion: Substitute butter for parve margarine to serve this dessert after a milk meal. This recipe doubles easily. Use a 9×12-inch pan and bake for 35 minutes.

This brownie recipe is not only one of my favorites, but a favorite of my children as well. I believe that their children and their children's children will love the taste of Bubbie's brownies in the years to come. This recipe is that good. Way to go, Mom!

INGREDIENTS

¾ cup flour

1 teaspoon baking powder

½ teaspoon salt

½ cup butter or parve margarine, softened

½ cup white sugar

1 cup brown sugar

2 eggs, beaten

1 teaspoon vanilla

½ cup chopped pecans

1 cup chocolate chips

Nonstick spray

1. Preheat the oven to 350 degrees. Grease a 9×9-inch pan.

2. In a mixing bowl, combine the flour, baking powder, and salt. In another mixing bowl, cream the butter. Add the white sugar, brown sugar, eggs, and vanilla to the butter. Slowly add the flour mixture to the butter mixture.

3. Stir in the chopped nuts and chocolate chips to the mixing bowl.

4. Spread the batter in the prepared pan. Bake for 35 minutes. Let cool and cut into squares.

Bon Bon Cookies

Yield: 20–25 servings

INGREDIENTS
½ cup parve margarine or butter
¾ cup confectioner's sugar
½ teaspoon vanilla or almond extract
1½ cup flour
1/8 teaspoon salt
1 jar (16 ounce) maraschino cherries or 2 cups Macadamia nuts
Chocolate icing (optional)

1. Preheat the oven to 350 degrees.

2. Mix the parve margarine, white sugar, and vanilla together in a mixing bowl. Slowly stir in the flour and salt while mixing.

3. Place each ball of dough on a baking sheet, spacing the cookies about 1 inch apart. Press 1 cherry or nut in the center of each dough ball. Bake for 12 to 15 minutes, cookies should be set, but not brown.

4. When the cookies are cool, dip the tops in chocolate icing.

Substitute butter for parve margarine to serve this dessert after a milk meal.

For chocolate dough, add 1 ounce unsweetened melted chocolate to the batter. For brown sugar dough, substitute the confectioner's sugar with ½ cup brown sugar.

Seven Layer Cookie Bars

Yield: 24 servings

Serving Suggestion: Serve this dessert after a milk meal, or have as a sweet midafternoon snack.

INGREDIENTS
¼ cup butter, melted
1 cup graham cracker crumbs
3½ cups flaked coconut
1 (6 ounce) bag chocolate chips
1 (6 ounce) bag butterscotch chips
1 (14 ounce) can sweetened condensed milk
1 cup chopped nuts

1. Preheat the oven to 325 degrees. Pour the butter in a 9×12-inch pan.

2. Press the graham cracker crumbs in an even layer at the bottom of the pan. Layer flaked coconut, chocolate chips, and butterscotch chips in the pan. Pour the sweetened condensed milk evenly over the other ingredients. Top with the nuts.

3. Bake for 30 minutes. Let cool then cut the bars into squares.

Date-Nut Fingers

Yield: 6–8 servings

INGREDIENTS

2 eggs

2 cups confectioner's sugar,
  plus more for dusting

½ teaspoon vanilla

½ cup all purpose flour

1 teaspoon baking powder

½ teaspoon salt

1 cup chopped nuts

1 cup chopped dates

Nonstick spray

1. Preheat the oven to 325 degrees. Grease an 8×8-inch pan.

2. In a mixing bowl, beat eggs until foamy. Stir in the confectioner's sugar and vanilla.

3. In a separate bowl, mix the flour, baking powder, and salt. Stir in the egg mixture. Stir in the nuts and dates. Pour the batter into the prepared pan.

4. Bake for 25 to 30 minutes or until the top has a dull crust. Cut into long rectangles. Roll each one in confectioner's sugar while still warm.

Powdered Sweetness

Yield: 4–6 servings

INGREDIENTS

2 eggs
1 cup confectioner's sugar,
    plus more for dusting
½ teaspoon vanilla
1 teaspoon almond extract
½ cup flour
1 teaspoon baking powder

½ teaspoon salt
½ cup chopped nuts
1 cup chopped dates
½ cup butterscotch chips
½ cup chocolate chips
Nonstick spray

1. Preheat the oven to 325 degrees. Grease the baking sheet.

2. In a mixing bowl, beat the eggs until foamy. Stir in the confectioner's sugar, vanilla, and almond extract.

3. In a separate bowl, combine the flour, baking powder, and salt. Stir in the egg mixture.

4. Stir in the nuts, dates, butterscotch chips, and chocolate chips.

5. Shape the dough into balls. Place on a greased baking sheet 1 inch apart.

6. Bake for 15 to 20 minutes. When cool enough to handle, roll each one in confectioner's sugar.

I confess that this is one of those happy accident recipes. While shooting food photos, I realized that I needed a dessert. I checked around the kitchen for a recipe and came up with this classic of Bubbie's. The crew loved them, and I know you will too!

No Name Cake

Yield: 6–8 servings

Serving Suggestion: Serve this cake after either a milk or meat meal!

Bake this cake faster by pouring the mixture 9×12-inch pan. Bake at 325 degrees for 30 minutes.

INGREDIENTS

1 cup flour

1 cup white sugar

1 teaspoon baking soda

¾ cup nuts

1 egg

1 (8.5 ounce) can fruit cocktail, drained

1 teaspoon salt

1. Preheat the oven to 350 degrees.

2. In a bowl, mix all the ingredients together. Pour the mixture into a 10-inch pie plate.

3. Bake for 1 hour. Let cool before serving.

Raisin & Date Oatmeal Cookies

Yield: 6–8 servings

Serving Suggestion: Serve with a big glass of cold milk!

INGREDIENTS

1 cup flour

½ teaspoon salt

1 teaspoon baking soda

1 cup parve margarine,
    or butter if serving with a milk meal

1 cup white sugar

1 cup packed brown sugar

2 large eggs

1 teaspoon vanilla

4 cups quick cooking oats

1 cup chopped pitted dates

1 cup raisins

½ cup chopped pecans

Nonstick spray

1. Preheat the oven to 350 degrees. Grease a baking sheet.

2. In a small bowl, combine the flour, salt, and baking soda. In another separate mixing bowl, cream together the parve margarine, white sugar, and brown sugar. Stir in the eggs and vanilla. Beat the mixture until fluffy.

3. Add the flour mixture to the margarine mixture. Stir in the oats. When the oats are incorporated, stir in dates, raisins, and nuts. Drop the dough by teaspoons onto the baking sheet.

4. Bake for 8 to 10 minutes. Cool on waxed paper or a cooling rack.

Banana Bread

Yield: 8–10 servings

INGREDIENTS
2 eggs
½ cup butter
2 cups chopped nuts
2 cups flour
3 ripened bananas, mashed
1 cup white sugar
1 teaspoon baking soda
½ teaspoon salt
½ teaspoon cinnamon
Nonstick spray

1. Preheat the oven to 350 degrees. Grease an 8×8-inch pan.

2. In a large bowl, combine all the ingredients together. Pour the batter into the prepared pan. Bake for 45 minutes.

3. Run a knife around the edge of the pan. Put a plate upside down covering the top of the pan. Flip the pan and the plate over. Remove the pan, leaving the bread on the plate. Place a cooling rack on top of the bread. Flip the rack and the plate over so the bread rests on the cooling rack. Let the bread cool before slicing.

Beer Bread

Yield: 8–10 servings

INGREDIENTS
3 cups self-rising flour
1 (12 ounce) can beer,
    at room temperature
2 eggs
2 tablespoons white sugar
Nonstick spray

1. Preheat oven to 350 degrees.
    Grease a 9-inch loaf pan.

2. In a large bowl, combine all the
    ingredients together. Pour the batter
    into the prepared pan.

3. Allow the bread to stand for 15 to 20
    minutes. Bake for 1 hour.

Cranberry Bread

Yield: 8–10 servings

Serving suggestion: Substitute butter for parve margarine if serving the bread with a milk meal.

INGREDIENTS

1 cup whole cranberry sauce
1 egg, beaten
1 teaspoon grated orange rind
2 tablespoons parve margarine or butter, melted
2 cups flour
½ cup white sugar

3 teaspoons baking powder
1 teaspoon salt
¼ teaspoon baking soda
1 teaspoon cinnamon
½ cup chopped nuts
Nonstick spray

1. Preheat the oven to 350 degrees. Grease a 5×9-inch pan.

2. In a large mixing bowl, combine the cranberry sauce, egg, orange rind, and margarine.

3. In a separate mixing bowl, combine the flour, white sugar, baking powder, salt, baking soda, and cinnamon. Gradually add the flour mixture to the cranberry mixture. Stir in the nuts.

4. Pour the batter into the prepared pan. Bake for 45 to 50 minutes. Let cool before slicing.

BUBBIE'S JEWISH RECIPES

*E*very Bubbie has her own recipes, recipes that have been handed
down from her mother and her mother's mother. Growing up, I
remember all the wonderful smells emanating from my mother's
kitchen while she made these recipes. She loved to entertain with style
and plenty of food.

*The most important meal and biggest family gathering every year has
always been held on Passover. My mom would cook for days to prepare
one feast, the Seder, on the first night of Passover. During and after the
meal many songs were sung and traditions followed. The memories I
made during those meals are some of the happiest of my life growing up.*

*The treasured recipes in this section remind me of that time and that
being Jewish is more than prayer. It is a lifestyle and food plays an
important role. Whether you live the Jewish lifestyle or not, these recipes
should transport you to a time when you were surrounded by family and
filled feelings of happiness and love. Hopefully, the spirit in these foods
will be kept alive for generations to come. Now that's comfort food!*

Chopped Liver

 SONG PAIRING: "My Yiddishe Mama."

Yield: 4–8 servings

Serving Suggestion:
Serve on crackers or toasted bread.

INGREDIENTS
2 pounds beef liver, broiled or pan fried
4 hard-boiled eggs
2 onions
1/3 cup schmaltz (chicken fat)
2 tablespoons mayonnaise
1 teaspoon salt
1 teaspoon ground black pepper

> ### FOR PASSOVER
>
> *Song pairings for Passover: "Let My People Go," "Ma Nishtana," and "Daye'nu"*
>
> *Check out my version of these songs on my website!*

1. In a blender or food processor, combine the beef liver, eggs, and onions. Blend together. Remove the blended contents to a mixing bowl.

2. Stir in the schmaltz, mayonnaise, salt, pepper, and ½ cup water.

3. Chill for 1 hour.

Tzimmes

Yield: 4 servings

Serving Suggestion: Bubbie recommends serving Tzimmes with brisket or cooked chicken.

INGREDIENTS

2 teaspoons olive oil

4–6 carrots, thinly sliced

4 tablespoons brown sugar

¼ cup pineapple juice

Salt and white pepper to taste

2 slices of canned pineapple
   cut into pieces

1 mango, cubed

½ teaspoon nutmeg

½ teaspoon cinnamon

1. In a large saucepan, warm the oil over low heat. Stir in the carrots. Cook the carrots for 10 to 15 minutes. The cooked carrots should be firm but not crunchy.

2. Stir in the brown sugar, pineapple juice, salt, and white pepper.

3. Simmer over low heat for 10 minutes. Stir in the pineapple, mango and cinnamon. Simmer for another 5 minutes. Remove from heat. Serve warm as a side dish.

Bubbie's Sweet Matzah Kugel

Yield: 4–6 servings

INGREDIENTS

8 matzahs, crumbled
4 tart apples, shredded
½ cup white sugar
½ teaspoon salt
¼ teaspoon cinnamon
½ cup chopped nuts
½ cup seedless raisins
6 eggs
1 orange rind or lemon rind, grated

Topping
¼ teaspoon grated orange rind,
    or lemon rind
1 teaspoon brown sugar or white sugar

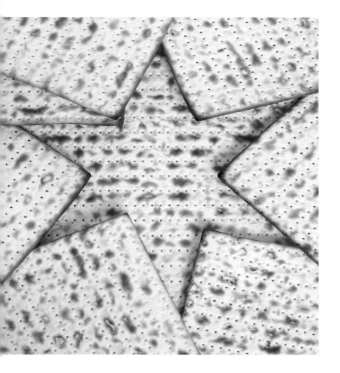

1. Preheat the oven to 325 degrees.
    Grease a 9×9-inch pan.

2. Place the matzah in a bowl of
    warm water for 2 minutes. Drain
    the water out of the bowl leaving
    the matzah.

3. Stir in the apples, white sugar,
    salt, cinnamon, nuts, and raisins
    into the bowl. Mix the ingredi-
    ents thoroughly. Add the eggs
    to the bowl. Mix the ingredients
    together. Pour the mixture in the
    prepared pan.

4. Bake for 30 to 35 minutes. Let cool
    for 5 to 10 minutes. Top with the
    grated orange and brown sugar.

Matzah Brei

Yield: 4–6 servings

INGREDIENTS
4 matzahs
4 eggs, beaten
2 tablespoons parve margarine
honey or brown sugar, to taste

1. Break matzah into small pieces. Put the matzah in a bowl of warm water for 2 minutes. Drain the water out of the bowl leaving the matzah.

2. Add the eggs to the bowl of matzah.

3. In a pan, melt the parve margarine over medium high heat. Fry the matzah until it is golden brown, about 2 to 3 minutes. Top with honey or brown sugar.

Matzah Balls for Soup

My Bubbie used to render the schmaltz for her recipes. It took forever. Today we can buy it in the grocery. Hurrah!

Yield: 4–6 servings

INGREDIENTS

1 egg
4 tablespoons schmaltz (chicken fat)
½ cup chicken stock
1 cup matzah meal

½ teaspoon salt
½ teaspoon ground black pepper
1 tablespoon parsley
2 tablespoons onion powder

1. In a medium mixing bowl, whisk the egg. Add the schmaltz, chicken stock, matzah meal, salt, pepper, parsley, and onion power to the bowl. Mix the ingredients thoroughly. Cover the bowl with plastic wrap. Chill for 30 minutes.

2. In a large pot, boil 6 cups of water over high heat.

3. Make 1½-inch balls from the chilled matzah mixture. Place the balls in the boiling water.

4. Reduce the heat to medium low, cover the pot, and simmer for 15 minutes.

5. Remove the matzah balls and add them to your favorite soup stock.

Bubbie's Club Mix

 SONG PAIRING: "Papriosen," one of Bubbie's favorite Yiddish songs from years ago.

Yield: 4–6 servings

Serving Suggestion: Bubbie's Club Mix can be served by itself, over rice, or over pasta.

You can substitute kosher chuck steak or turkey for the chicken.

INGREDIENTS

3–4 kosher chicken breasts
½ head cabbage, shredded
2 onions, chopped
1 pound frozen mixed vegetables
1 cup uncooked rice
¼ cup oil
1 teaspoon salt
2 teaspoons ground black pepper

FOR SHABBAT AND OTHER HOLIDAYS

Song Pairing: "Bim Bam," "L'cha Dodi" and "Ydid Nefesh."

Shabbat songs Bubbie loves! Check out my versions on the website.

1. Preheat the oven to 375 degrees.

2. Wash the chicken under cold water. Pat to dry. Dice the chicken.

3. In a 9×12-inch pan, combine the chicken, 2 cups water, and all remaining ingredients. Stir the mixture together.

4. Bake covered for 1 hour. Stir the mixture every 15 minutes.

Potato Pancakes Latkes for Hanukkah

SONG PAIRING: "Oh Hanukkah" and "Ma'oz Tzur." Check out my versions on the website.

Yield: 4–6 servings

INGREDIENTS

2 eggs

1 teaspoon salt

1 tablespoon basil

4 large potatoes, grated

1 scallion or a leek, grated

1½ teaspoons baking powder

½ cup flour

1 tablespoon butter

¼ cup applesauce
    or sour cream (optional)

1. In a mixing bowl, whisk the eggs. Whisk in the salt and basil. Stir in the potatoes and scallions.

2. Stir in the baking powder and flour. Mix the ingredients together thoroughly to form the batter.

3. In a sauté pan, melt the butter over medium heat. Using about ¼ cup batter make small pancakes in the pan. Fry the pancakes for about 3 minutes on each side. Drain the pancakes on brown paper or paper towels.

4. To keep warm, spread the pancakes out on a baking sheet. Bake for 2 to 3 minutes at 375 degrees. Before serving top with applesauce or sour cream.

Tarnegolet Bemizt Hadarim
(Hebrew for "Chicken in Citrus Juice")

 SONG PAIRING: "Tumbalalaika," a Yiddish folk song.

Yield: 4–6 servings

Serving Suggestion: Serve with apple slices, strawberries, blueberries, and nuts.

INGREDIENTS

3–4 kosher chicken breasts

1 tablespoon ground black pepper

1 cup fresh orange juice

2 tablespoons fresh lemon juice

¼ cup honey

2 tablespoons chopped chili peppers

1 cup chopped apricots

1 lemon or orange, sliced

1. Preheat oven to 375 degrees. Wash the chicken. Pat it dry.

2. Sprinkle the chicken with ground black pepper. Arrange the chicken in a layer, skin side down, in a baking dish.

3. In a small bowl, stir the chili peppers, orange juice, lemon juice, and honey together. Pour the mixture over the chicken until it's well moistened.

4. Bake the chicken for 15 minutes. Turn the chicken over, adding the apricots on the top. Bake for 30 minutes. Baste the chicken with the juices from the pan every 10 minutes. Arrange the chicken on plates with lemon or orange slices.

Sweet Noodle Kugel

Yield: 6–10 servings

Serving Suggestion: Sprinkle a thin layer of Ricotta cheese on the finished kugel for added flavor.

INGREDIENTS
1 (16 ounce) bag of noodles
½ cup parve margarine or butter
4 eggs
1 cup brown sugar
1 tablespoon vanilla
1½ cups applesauce or crushed pineapple, drained
1 teaspoon cinnamon
1 teaspoon nutmeg

1. Preheat the oven to 350 degrees.

2. Cook the noodles according to the package directions. Drain the noodles in a colander. Put the noodles into a large mixing bowl.

3. Stir in the margarine while the noodles while are still warm. Stir in the eggs, brown sugar, applesauce, vanilla, cinnamon, and nutmeg.

4. Put the mixture into a 9×13-baking pan. Cover with aluminum foil. Bake for 30 minutes. Uncover the kugel. Bake for another 20 to 30 minutes.

Kreplach

Yield: 8–10 servings

INGREDIENTS

4 tablespoons olive oil

2 pounds lean kosher ground beef

3 onions, diced

½ teaspoon ground black pepper

1 teaspoon garlic powder

1½ teaspoon salt

2 cups flour

2 eggs

1½ cups warm water

Replace the beef with chicken or make vegetarian kreplach using vegetable ingredients in place of the meat.

1. In a large skillet, heat the oil over medium heat. When hot, stir in the beef, onions, pepper, garlic powder, and ½ teaspoon salt. Cook until beef is browned, about 10 minutes.

2. In a large mixing bowl, combine flour, eggs, and the remaining salt. Mix until dough is smooth. Roll the dough into a ball.

3. On a floured board, roll out the dough until it is ¼ inch thick. Cut the dough into 2 inch squares.

4. Place a spoonful of the meat mixture in the center of each square. Fold the dough in half diagonally, forming a triangle. Put a bit of warm water along the edges. Pinch the edges to seal them together.

5. Bring a large pot water to a boil. Carefully drop each kreplach into the water. Cook for 4 minutes or until they float to the top.

6. Remove each kreplach with a slotted spoon and serve.

SONGS

Available on the websites: **cantormitch.com** or **koshercuisine.com**.
Hear Cantor Mitch singing his favorite Jewish and Family songs.

SHABBAT SONGS
Bim Bam
Ma Yafeh Hayom
L'cha Dodi
Ydid Nefesh

HANUKKAH SONGS
Ma'oz Tzur
Oh Hanukkah
Mi Yimalel

PASSOVER SONGS
Let My People Go
Ma Nishtana
Daye'nu

FAMILY SONGS BY CANTOR MITCH
Hine Mah Tov—Music by Cantor Mitch
Shir Mishpacha—Lyrics and music by Cantor
   Mitch
Family Blessing—Music by Cantor Mitch, words
   by Siddur

All songs copyright Cantor Mitch Publishing

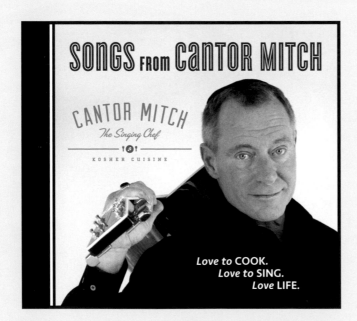

Subject Index

Alfredo sauce
    with fish, 67
    premade, 99
    with vegetables, 89
apricot chicken, 49
artificial sweeteners, as parve, 4
Asian foods/flavors, 74, 97. *See also*
    Chinese foods/flavors
asparagus soup, 30
avocado
    brochette, 19
    salad, 107, 111

baked goods
    bars, 136, 137
    breads, 143, 144, 145
    cakes, 140
    cookies, 135, 136, 139, 141
    for meat meals, 140
    for milk meals, 133, 135, 136, 149,
       145
    recipes for, 131–145
    banana bread, 131, 143
bars, 133, 136, 137
beef. *See also* meat
    beef liver, 148
    brisket, 41
    ground beef, 37, 39, 43

recipes for, 33–43
    steak, 35
beer bread, 144
black bean soup, 26
blessings. *See* brachot
blonde brownies, 133
bon-bon cookies, 135
brachot
    definition of, 2, 4
    for specific foods/meals, 6–7
bread
    brachot for, 6
    starter, 19
    sweet, 143, 144, 145
breaded zucchini, 18
brisket, 33, 34, 41
broccoli
    quiche, 83
    side dish, 89
    simply cooked, 19
    soup, 31
brochette, 19
burgers, 39

cake, 140
chai tea sorbet, 129
cheese
    quiche, 81, 83
    starter, 13

chicken
    as beef substitution, 157
    entrées, 45–59, 153
    grilling of, 59
    kosher laws for, 45
    kosher skinless breasts, 45
    recipes for, 45–59
    rinsing of kosher meat, 45
    salad, 112
    soup, 27
chicken a l'orange, 47
chicken florentine, 53
chicken marsala, 51
chicken salad, 112
chili, 43
Chinese foods/flavors, 17. *See also*
    Asian foods/flavors
chocolate
    cookie, 135
    pie, 121
citrus chicken, 47, 155
club mix, 153
cookies, 135, 136, 139, 141
cranberry bread, 145
cream of asparagus soup, 30
cream of mushroom soup, 23
curry chicken, 58

dairy products. *See* milk/dairy
    products
date bars/cookies, 137, 139, 141
dessert
    baked goods, 131–145
    for chicken entrées, 45
    for meat meals, 119, 121, 140
    for milk meals, 116, 117, 118, 119,
        121, 124, 133, 135, 136, 149, 145

pies, 115–121
    sorbets, 123–129
dietary laws, 4. *See also* Kashrut
drinks, brachot for, 7

egg dishes. *See* quiche
egg rolls, 17
eggplant, 92, 93
entrées
    chicken, 45–59
    fish, 61–77
    meat, 33–43
    purposes of, 33
    quiche, 79–87
    vegetables, 88–97

first course. *See* starters
fish
    cooking methods for, 61, 67, 69
    eating with milk/dairy products, 4
    entrées, 61–77
    garnishes for, 73
    health benefits of, 61
    kosher laws for, 61, 99
    popularity of, 61
    sauces for, 65, 73, 99
    recipes for, 61–77
    soup, 29
fleishig, definition of 4. *See also* meat
forbidden foods. *See* Kashrut
French silk pie, 121
fruit
    brachot for, 7
    breads, 143, 145
    cake, 140
    pies, 116, 117, 118
    salads, 111, 113

sorbets, 125, 126, 127, 128
starters, 13, 19

garlic sauce, 100
garnishes, kosher laws for, 15
gazpacho, 28
gelatin salad, 113
graham cracker piecrusts, 115. *See also*
    piecrusts
grain products, brachot for, 6
green beans, 97
grilling
    chicken, 59
    fish, 72
guava sorbet, 127

Hanukkah, 154, 158
health
    and eating fish, 61
    and kosher diet, 4
heckcher, and premade foods, 3, 81.
    See also premade foods
herb
    garlic sauce, 100
    salad, 108
herbs de Provence, 24
hollandaise sauce, 89, 105

Italian foods/flavors, 75

Jewish lifestyle, 147. *See also* kosher
    foods; traditional Jewish foods

Kashrut, definition of, 4. *See also*
    kosher foods
key lime pie, 118
kosher, definition of, 4

kosher foods
    and cooking philosophy, 2–3
    and health, 4
    laws for, 4
    purpose of, 4
    traditional, 3. *See also* traditional
        Jewish foods
kreplach, 157
kugel, 150, 156

lasagna, 94, 95
latkes, 154
layered cookie bars, 136
liqueur, in sorbet, 124
liver, 148
lox quiche, 87

main course. *See* entrées
mango sorbet, 128
margarine, as parve, 4
marinades
    for chicken, 47, 49, 51, 59
    for fish, 62
marmalade, with vegetables, 89, 91
matzah
    balls, 152
    brei, 151
    kugel, 150
meat. *See also* beef
    availability of kosher meat, 33–34
    cooking methods for, 35
    entrées, 33–43, 157
    kosher laws for, 4, 11, 15, 33, 34, 45,
        89, 99
    rinsing of kosher meat, 34
    substitutions for, 153, 157
meatballs, 36

milchig, definition of 4. *See also* milk/
    dairy products, kosher laws for
milk/dairy products
    kosher laws for, 4, 11, 33, 115, 118
    starters, 11
mushroom
    quiche, 85
    soup, 23
    starter, 15
music
    and family, 5, 147
    song list, 158
    and spirituality, 2, 3, 147

niçoise salad, 110
noodle kugel, 156

orange sorbet, 126

parve, definition of, 4
Passover, 147, 148, 158
peach pie, 116
pear pie, 117
pecan pie, 119
pepper steak, 35
pesto
    with chicken, 55
    with fish, 69
    premade, 99
pie
    kosher laws for, 115
    popularity of, 115
    premade crusts, 81, 115
    recipes for, 115–121
pineapple and coconut sorbet, 129
potato pancake latkes, 154

premade foods
    convenience of, 3, 115, 152
    heckcher labeling of, 3, 81
presentation, of food, 9

quiche
    basic recipe for, 81
    cheeses for, 81
    definition of, 79
    entrées, 79–87
    kosher laws for, 81
    recipes for, 79–87
    serving suggestions for, 79, 81

raisin cookies, 141
rice
    club mix, 153
    with beef, 37
    with chicken, 51
    wild, 51

salad
    cutting/chopping of, 107
    recipes for, 107–113
salmon, 73, 74, 75
salsa, with chicken, 57
sauce
    kosher laws for, 99
    premade vs. scratch, 99
    recipes for, 99–105
schmaltz, premade, 152
Seder, 147
Shabbat, 41, 153, 158
side dishes
    salads as. *See* salads
    vegetables as, 89, 91, 97. *See also*
        vegetables

snapper, 71, 72
sole, 62, 63
sorbet
      guidelines for, 124
      kosher option, 123
      for milk meal, 124
      recipes for, 123–129
soup
      cream-based, 23, 30, 31
      popularity of, 21
      presentation of, 21
      recipes for, 21–31
      stock-based, 24, 25, 26, 27, 28, 29
Spanish foods/flavors, 57, 70
spinach
      with chicken, 53
      with fish, 71
      quiche, 85
      salad, 109
spirituality
      and food, 3, 4, 99, 147
      and music, 2, 3
starters
      bread, 19
      cheese, 13
      fruit, 13, 19
      kosher laws for, 11
      as meals, 11
      popularity of, 11
      purposes of, 11
      recipes for, 11–19
      vegetables, 12, 15, 17, 18
strawberry sorbet, 125
string beans, 97
stuffed mushrooms, 15
sweet and sour meatballs, 36

Tarnegolet bemizt hadarim, 155
tilapia, 65, 67, 69, 70
tomato soups, 24, 28
traditional Jewish foods
      and Jewish lifestyle, 147
      and music, 147
      recipes for, 147–157
turkey, as meat substitution, 153
Tzimmes, 149

vegetable soup, 24
vegetables
      brachot for, 7
      cooking methods for, 89, 91
      cutting/trimming of, 91
      entrées, 89, 92, 93, 95, 157
      kosher laws for, 11, 89, 99
      leftovers, 25
      popularity of, 89
      quiche, 82, 83
      recipes for, 89–97
      sauces for, 89, 91, 99
      side dishes, 89, 91, 97. See also
            salads
      soups, 23, 24, 25, 28, 30, 31
      starters, 12, 15, 17, 18
vegetarian, kosher laws for, 11, 89
vichyssoise, 29

walleye, 77
white sauce, 102
wine and grape juice, brachot for, 7
wine sauce, 101

zucchini
      quiche, 82
      starter, 18

Song Index

"Ain't She Sweet?" 36
"America" (*West Side Story*), 28
"Artza Alinu," 82
"As Time Goes By" (*Casablanca*), 95

"Bali Ha'i" (*South Pacific*), 17
"Be Our Guest" (*Beauty and the Beast*), 58
"Bim Bam," 158

"Cabaret" (*Cabaret*), 29
"Chicago" (*Chicago*), 35

"Daye'nu," 148, 158
"Dixie," 23

"Family Blessing," 158

"Goldfinger" (*Goldfinger*), 65
"Good Day Sunshine," 81

"Hava Nagila!" 82
"Here Comes the Sun," 83
"Hine Mah Tov," 158

"I Get a Kick Out of You," 37
"It's a Puzzlement" (*The King and I*), 97

"L'cha Dodi," 158
"La Bamba," 70
"Let My People Go," 148, 158

"Ma Nishtana," 148, 158
"Ma Yafeh Hayom," 158
"Ma'oz Tzur," 154, 158
"Macarena," 57
"Man Without Love, A," 53
"Maria" (*West Side Story*), 75
"Moonlight in Vermont," 24
"My Yiddishe Mama," 148

"Nel blu dipinto di blu," 55
"Non più andrai" (*The Marriage of Figaro*), 51

"O Sole Mio," 67
"Oh Hanukkah," 154
"Oh My Papa," 39
"Oh, What a Beautiful Mornin'" (*Oklahoma*), 12
"Over the Rainbow" (*Wizard of Oz*), 25

"Papriosen," 153
Popeye the Sailor Man (theme song), 85

"Quando Quando Quando," 69

"Sailing," 71
"Se vuol ballere" (*The Marriage of Figaro*), 51
"Shabbat Prayer" (*Fiddler on the Roof*), 41
"Shall We Dance?" (*The King and I*), 93
"Shir Mishpacha," 158
"Sittin' on the Dock of the Bay," 62
"Something Wonderful" (*The King and I*), 74
"Summertime" (*Porgy and Bess*), 49
"Sweet Home Alabama," 72

"That's Amore," 15
"Tradition" (*Fiddler on the Roof*), 27
"Tumbalalaika," 155

"Volare," 55

"When the Saints Go Marching In," 26
"Wreck of the Edmond Fitzgerald, The," 73

"Ydid Nefesh," 158
"Yellow Submarine," 63
"Young at Heart," 77

Acknowledgments

Within every creative work there are people who stand beside you and believe in what you are doing.

I have found that in writing *Kosher Cuisine for a New Generation*, it has been no different for me. I would like to acknowledge:

TACY MANGAN, producer, writer and director, for her knowledge and insight;

NANCY TUMINELLY, Mighty Media and Scarletta, for her guidance through the whole process;

BRENDA PIEKARSKI, Adventure Films, producer, web designer and photographer, for her creative skills;

MATTHEW WITCHELL and ADRIAN DANCIU, photographers, for their beautiful photos and attention to detail;

This book would not be possible without their friendship and expert help.

CANTOR MITCH
The Singing Chef

KOSHER CUISINE

Biography

CANTOR MITCHELL KOWITZ started working with food in his early twenties as a vegetable cutter. He progressed to a prep chef and then a sous chef over a ten-year period while in New York City. While working on his cooking skills he was also performing off Broadway and later attended Cantorial school. He is the proud father of three children, Joshua, Shelly, and Michael. He has served two congregations in his twenty-five years as a Cantor. Cantor Mitch has also written many songs due to his love of music. He lives in St. Paul, Minnesota where he continues to serve the Jewish community in a variety of ways.